D1795027

Citizenship Education in
Conflict-Affected Areas

Also available from Bloomsbury

Civics and Citizenship Education in Australia,
Andrew Peterson and Libby Tudball
Global Citizenship Education and the Crises of Multiculturalism,
Massimiliano Tarozzi and Carlos Alberto Torres
Peace Education, edited by Monisha Bajaj and Maria Hantzopoulos

Citizenship Education in Conflict-Affected Areas

Lebanon and Beyond

Bassel Akar

BLOOMSBURY ACADEMIC
LONDON • NEW YORK • OXFORD • NEW DELHI • SYDNEY

BLOOMSBURY ACADEMIC
Bloomsbury Publishing Plc
50 Bedford Square, London, WC1B 3DP, UK
1385 Broadway, New York, NY 10018, USA

BLOOMSBURY, BLOOMSBURY ACADEMIC and the Diana logo are
trademarks of Bloomsbury Publishing Plc

First published in Great Britain 2019

ISBN: HB: 978-1-4742-9836-0
         ePDF: 978-1-4742-9838-4
         eBook: 978-1-4742-9837-7

Typeset by Integra Software Services Pvt. Ltd.
Printed and bound in Great Britain

To find out more about our authors and books visit www.bloomsbury.com
and sign up for our newsletters.

Contents

Acknowledgements vi
A Note on Transliteration and Style vii

Introduction 1

Part One Education for Active Citizenship in Areas Affected by Conflict

1 Education for Development and Social Reconstruction 9
2 Constructing Ideals of Citizenship for Living Together 25
3 Effective Learning for Active Citizenship 47

Part Two Citizenship Education in Lebanon in Rhetoric and Reality

4 Lebanon: Education Policy in Times of Conflict and Change 69
5 Young People: Their Citizenship, Their Learning 83
6 Teachers: Teaching Civics 103

Part Three Pedagogies in Conflict

7 Undermining Active Citizenship 127
8 Transforming Civics and Conflict 139

Bibliography 148
Index 166

Acknowledgements

I extend my gratitude to Professor Hugh Starkey, at the University College London Institute of Education, who provided technical support in producing instruments that engaged the students as citizens with a voice, unparalleled guidance on reading citizenship studies and, most importantly, inspiration. All of the school visits were possible because of the school heads' vote of confidence and enthusiasm in research on learning citizenship in school. I especially thank all the teachers and students who participated and continued discussions even outside the classroom. I am also grateful to Notre Dame University – Louaize for the semester sabbatical leave to write this manuscript.

A Note on Transliteration and Style

In some places, certain Arabic words were kept to either preserve their meanings or draw on their derivatives. These Arabic terms are in italics with definitions using their English synonyms. Arabic terms are presented in English letters and in italics by following the guidelines of the *International Journal of Middle East Studies* Transliteration System for Arabic, Persian and Turkish. Finally, Arabic is the main language of the classrooms where data was gathered from. Students and teachers were able to choose between instruments in English or Arabic. All transcriptions and responses were translated into Arabic. A sample of translated responses and transcribed interviews was back-translated for accuracy.

Introduction

Kosovo, Rwanda, Northern Ireland, Lebanon, Nepal, Bosnia and Herzegovina, South Africa, Guatemala and Sri Lanka have very little in common. They have, however, endured periods of armed conflict after the Second World War that resulted in mass killings, kidnappings and other extreme violations of human life. Although their governments declared their wars as over, the reverberations of armed conflict and its roots manifest in ongoing tensions, structural violence and collective memory. The governments of these countries have also turned to education as an approach for social reconstruction, preventing future conflicts and empowering a new generation of people who could live together in more peaceful, just, collaborative and inclusive ways.

When transitioning out of armed conflict, stakeholders in government institutions, civil society organizations and international agencies invest great efforts (not necessarily money) in quickly trying to rebuild and reform education. Post-war reconstruction of education involves rebuilding its infrastructures that were either destroyed or transformed into prisons or shelters. Education reform aims at redesigning a blueprint for sustainable peace and human development. Stakeholders assume that education will support the generation of young people to process and reconcile themselves to the social and psychological aftermaths of war. They also assume that education can foster a community at school for children to grow up as citizens who actively promote social justice, non-violence and human rights. However, the actual design and development of education policy is typically challenged by the political aftermaths of armed conflict. Moreover, translating policy into practice by transforming approaches to learning and teaching is even further challenged by cultures of pedagogy established before and during conflict.

Lebanon hosts a diversity of 4 million Lebanese across 18 official sects, over 1.3 million Syrian and 455,000 Palestinian refugees and an estimated 200,000 domestic workers mainly from India, Sri Lanka, the Philippines, Ethiopia, Bangladesh and Nepal. Within a context of diverse sectarian (religious and political) and ethnic identities, the communities in Lebanon have faced periods of armed conflict and political strife and continue to live through the instabilities of corruption, limited social services, unsustainable living and ongoing sectarian tensions. It is crucial to note that diversity here is used to illustrate a context of plurality and by no means suggest it as a causal factor for the following destructive conflicts.

After the identity-based 15-year armed conflict (1975–1989), the war-torn nation sustained a reconstruction period in the 1990s. At the turn of the twenty-first century, political tensions arose again to a critical level. Criticisms towards the role of Syria in Lebanon's politics led to the creation of an opposition party followed by a string of assassinations of prominent social and political figures. In 2005, a series of protests, dubbed the *Intifadāt al Istiqlāl*, or Independence Uprisings, led to the departure of Syrian troops from Lebanese territory. Soon after, in July 2006, Israel launched a 34-day offensive against Hezbollah, demolishing infrastructure across the country and communities in the southern suburbs of Beirut through air strikes. Only 1 year later, the Lebanese Army and Fatah al-Islam warred against each other, which resulted in the destruction of the Palestinian refugee camp Nahr el-Bared. Most recently, the sectarian shootings between two pocket communities in Tripoli in February 2012 also indicated the reverberations of the Syrian uprising to neighbouring Lebanon and raised further concern to the controversial issue of baring arms. Besides the obvious state of swinging between conflict and post-conflict statuses and deep-rooted social and political tensions, the active levels of engagement and leadership among young people in Lebanon have been less frequently acknowledged.

Young people in Lebanon and, more recently, the region of West Asia and North Africa have demonstrated a distinctively high level of political engagement in civil society campaigns against injustice and for the progress of democracy. In Lebanon, a culture of activism and communal identity has been predominant in the growth and influence of its civil society and the coalitions civil society has made with political parties, state actors and other civil society organizations (Härdig 2011). Moreover, during times of protest, political leaders have been seen as able to mobilize young supporters to the streets or calling on them to exercise restraint and control (see Samaha 2006). Indeed, youth activism in higher education institutions has become somewhat contentious since student government officers often represent political parties (Aboulissan 2011; Gambill 2003) while political activities such as elections and debates have broken out into violence (Bakri and Fattah 2007; The Daily Star 2011). Regionally, the world has witnessed the youth-led mobilization of people (e.g. through online social networks) to protest against dictatorial regimes in Tunisia, Egypt, Libya, Yemen, Algeria, Bahrain and Syria resulting in uprisings, armed conflicts and political change, which has been tagged as the Arab Spring.

The role of education can be most critical and problematic in conditions of armed conflict, political instability and reconstruction. Besides it being part of the solution, education can also be manipulated into a destructive force by being a cause for conflict (Smith and Vaux 2003), a mechanism for repression and exclusion such as denial of schooling (Bush and Saltarelli 2000) or as a place for [un]intended harm ranging from high frequencies of testing to rape (Harber 2004). Thus, the development of educational programmes for active citizenship require careful considerations of content, alignment, assessment, pedagogical approaches, resources and teacher education, to name a few. Finding out young people's conceptualizations of citizenship could better inform the design of citizenship education since it could address the youth's needs and identify opportunities to facilitate and contextualize learning. Moreover, finding out young peoples' individual understandings of citizenship and how they have been conceptualized could more accurately develop the aims and pedagogical approaches towards learning for active citizenship.

Citizenship Education in Conflict-Affected Areas: Lebanon and Beyond closely investigates the latter. How we learn and teach for citizenship largely determines the extent to which young people are indeed learning to live together. Also, how we learn and teach for citizenship is largely influenced by socially constructed understandings of citizenship and learning. This book examines the practices and influencing factors that shape classroom realities of learning and teaching the vision of citizenship prescribed in education policy. More critically, it challenges the extent to which existing practices and even policies of citizenship education are indeed helpful or harmful.

This book is organized into three parts. In Part One, each of the three chapters presents a theoretical variable for examining citizenship education for social reconstruction in conflict-affected areas. Chapter 1 introduces the fragility of areas affected by armed conflict and the extent to which provisions of education can engage people as active citizens who can either capitalize on cultural diversity or shape the curriculum, pedagogy and classroom into sources of harm. Showing the vulnerability of education is critical to the conclusion of this book, which will demonstrate the extent to which classroom pedagogies of citizenship education can indeed be harmful as well as beneficial. In Chapter 2, I define the type of citizenship that education in times of social reconstruction aims to foster and, especially, within the cultural context of Lebanon. I do this by approaching citizenship as a relationship between individuals and surrounding communities and examining the elements, dynamics and degrees that constitute this relationship. Ideals of citizenship are also drawn from early Islamic literature from the West Asia and North Africa region to investigate similarities and differences with established modern democratic ideals and underscore values unique to the region. Chapter 3 focuses on educational approaches to fostering active citizenship. While traditions of memorization have maintained a political hand over what and how young people learn, more dialogic and collaborative approaches are what empower young people to critically reflect on social injustices and celebrate the strengths of diversity.

Part Two of this book comprises another three chapters that juxtapose the policies and practices of citizenship education in Lebanon. In Chapter 4, I introduce Lebanon as a case study where the government consistently turns to education as an approach for social reconstruction after armed conflict and major political transformations, namely independence and the rise of pan-Arabism. Chapters 5 and 6 present narratives of citizenship and learning and teaching for citizenship from secondary school students and civics teachers, respectively. Teacher interviews and students' survey packs and class discussions took place in private schools, a sector that hosts over 70 per cent of the students in Lebanon. I also draw on observations from visits to civic education classrooms and conversations with civics teachers in public schools. The students' survey packs revealed, to a great extent, active and communitarian-based notions of citizenship and certain dynamics of citizenship like kinship and sacrifice that could conflict with human rights and democratic principles found in North American and West European constructs of citizenship. When reflecting on their classroom learning, they described dominant practices of rote learning and a prescriptive textbook as 'hypocritical'. The relationship between their constructs of 'good citizenship' and classroom learning experiences suggests that civil society and home are far more reliable and realistic spaces to live as active citizens than the civics classroom. The teacher interviews, on the other hand, revealed, for the most part, minimalist notions of citizenship that focus on a national consciousness demonstrated by patriotism and the knowledge of laws. A few teachers highlighted certain practices of successful dialogic activities and practices that helped manage emotions in the classroom. The challenges that the teachers explained showed far more complex roots that limit the facilitation of learning for active citizenship in the classroom.

Part Three concludes this book with two chapters. In Chapter 7, I synthesize the findings to corroborate themes that emerged from the teachers' and students' written descriptions and conversations. The findings illustrate a vicious cycle of how authoritarian-like pedagogies undermine the aims of a national curriculum. In this citizenship education catch-22, learning civics in the classroom withdraws children away from government institutions and closer to spaces that allow them to practice active notions of citizenship like civil society and family. The phenomena of teaching citizenship by transferring preset knowledge and knowing that similar approaches that deny young people from engaging in critical pedagogies is also common in other conflict-affected areas. Chapter 8 takes a look forward into transforming the pedagogical culture of knowledge transference in citizenship education to one that engages young people as active citizens living together inside the classroom by, for example, questioning social injustices and capitalizing on diversity. I draw on emerging studies reporting on teachers' stories of reimagining and transforming their approaches to learning active and maximal notions of citizenship inside the classroom. These studies demonstrate the role of high-impact teachers as effective curriculum makers and, in effect, change agents.

Part One

Education for Active Citizenship in Areas Affected by Conflict

Education for Development and Social Reconstruction

The design and provisions of citizenship education in a context of social reconstruction and peacebuilding are based on the assumption that the learners' experiences will enable them to live with other people in an inclusive, informed, equitable and collaborative manner. The vision 'to live with other people' or the education utopia of 'learning to live together' popularized by Delors et al. (1996) becomes an even more critical driver for development in areas struggling to emerge out of periods and cultures of destructive conflict. It is in these areas where education is extremely vulnerable to various forms of conflict. Therefore, how we understand the nature of the conflict is fundamental to defining the vision of citizenship and educational approaches to realizing that vision (Tawil and Harley 2004). Hence, we must define the context of areas affected by conflict in order to critically examine the significance, aims and practices of citizenship education in these areas, which I do in this chapter.

I contextualize conflict-affected areas within a period of transitioning out of destructive and violent conflict. During this extremely fragile state, communities maintain the deep-rooted threats and injustices that manifest into more subtle forms of violence; they can even easily fall back into armed violence. I then illustrate how, during this transition, education is approached as a lever for social reconstruction and development. Provisions of education, however, are vulnerable to the values and practices of people in power, such as teachers, parents and policymakers. Hence, the practices of learning and teaching citizenship are examined through a critical lens that views education as an approach that can destroy as much as it can build.

Defining conflict-affected areas

In education and development studies, sites that have experienced war or other forms of extreme violence and are working for sustainable peace are typically described as post-conflict, conflict-ridden or conflict-affected. Among these three, the description 'post-conflict' is probably most commonly used. Selected literature from an exhaustive list of references on education and conflict compiled by UNESCO IBE (2011) defines countries like Rwanda, Burundi, Sierra Leone and Cambodia in post-conflict contexts. Also, in Quaynor's (2012) literature review of citizenship education in post-conflict contexts, the sample of nation-states included Lebanon, South Africa, Argentina, Peru, Northern Ireland, Cyprus and Bosnia and Herzegovina. These countries have undoubtedly experienced armed conflict too long for any people and have also managed to sustain a relative degree of stability without armed violence. The status of 'post-conflict', however, may still appear quite vague, misleading and premature for most if not all these areas that continue to struggle with sustained structural violence, high levels of social and political tensions and occasional outbursts of armed violence. We also frequently see the term 'post-conflict' put in scare quotes, which suggest doubt and uncertainty.

The empirical field that I examine as 'conflict-affected' is defined by key elements of conflict dynamics. In this field, conflict-affected areas (1) have passed through periods of extreme violence like wars and armed struggles, (2) are fragile enough to fall back into periods or bursts of direct violence and (3) continue to cultivate latent forms of conflict through cultural and structural violence. Classical theories of conflict describe conflict in two sequential forms: building hostilities during a latent stage and then manifesting into overt expressions. During latency, people grow tense and feel neglected, abused and frustrated. People experience these subconscious feelings when they are exploited, repressed and marginalized through structural violence like routine forms of aggression and barriers to equality (Galtung 1969, 1996). These latent forms of social injustice are further legitimized by cultural violence like xenophobia, racism and sexism through art, literature, memorials, religion, symbols and knowledge production (Galtung 1990). Also during latency, actions by the oppressed are static mostly because the people have become habituated to the imbalances of power (Curle 1971). This state of habituated oppression explains why generations endured dictatorial regimes in Libya and Egypt before the most exasperated triggered political revolutions in these countries and across the Arab region. As soon as the realities of oppression, marginalization and other injustices are unveiled, conflict then manifests into constructive or destructive expressions. Constructive expressions like protests, advocacy campaigns and dialogues can create opportunities to strengthen relationships, co-construct new solutions and even agree to disagree. Destructive expressions, on the other hand, include what Galtung (1969) describes as direct violence. Probably the most extreme forms of direct violence are when human lives are taken away, such as ethnic cleansing, genocide and war.

While this book draws mostly on Lebanon as a case study, I also reflect on other countries as areas affected by conflict and continue to struggle in their transitions to sustainable peace. In modern-day Lebanon, the most destructive period of direct violence was arguably the complex mesh of civil wars between 1975 and 1990 that left an estimated 250,000 dead and 17,000 missing. Separatist rebellions in Northern Ireland and Sri Lanka fought an armed struggle against a larger nationalist regime resulting in a loss of over 3,500 lives during 30 years of 'The Troubles' in Northern Ireland (1968–1998) and 26 years of civil war in Sri Lanka (1983–2009) claiming an estimated 100,000 lives. The ethnic cleansing of Bosniaks (Bosnian Muslims) in the Bosnian war of 1992–1995 was declared a genocide by the United Nations following records of systematic killing. In Rwanda, the uncontested genocide of 800,000 people, mostly Tutsis, occurred over a span of 100 days from April to June 1994. Identity-based conflicts like these constructed feudal-like classes of citizenry giving conditional access to human and civil rights based on gender, religion, ethnicity and national identity. Fortunately, these areas have broken past the deadlock of direct violence and transitioned into a period of peacebuilding.

Conflict-affected areas are also characterized by their fragility and vulnerability to easily regress into bursts of direct violence. Lund (1996) presents a bell curve model of conflict that can be instrumental in mapping stages and intensities of violence starting with the latent stage, escalating to war and de-escalating through settlements and peacebuilding. Similar to more contemporary theorists of conflict analysis like Francis (2002) and Lederach (2005), Lund also recognizes that, along the lifeline of conflict, other episodes of direct violence can erupt and those that appear to terminate can also re-escalate. The dynamics of conflict can even skip stages across escalation and de-escalation (Dudouet 2006). So, even when conflict-affected areas are transitioning from negotiations, settlements and signing of peace treaties to peacebuilding initiatives, the nature of conflict's dynamic ebb and flow and outbursts of violence maintain these areas as fragile or unstable. More than 15 years after the end of the 1975–1990 civil wars in Lebanon, unresolved roots to conflict re-erupted into a string of politically motivated assassinations (2004–2008) and armed battles between the Lebanese army and Palestinian militias based in refugee camps in Lebanon. After the Troubles in Northern Ireland (1968–1998), the Real Irish Republican Army (IRA) formed a new coalition in 2012 and continued sporadic attacks through car bombs and shootings until 2017. The instability of conflict-affected areas caused by interruptions of direct violence during peacebuilding periods sustains a culture of war and violence. This continuity of armed conflict reinforces social divisions among groups that have engaged in armed struggles against each other.

A third characteristic of areas affected by conflict when contextualizing citizenship education is the continuity of latent conflict and structural and cultural violence during peacebuilding. Corruption, gender-based violence, illegalization of homosexuality, conservative approaches to nationalism and unsustainable management of resources, for example, may or may not be directly linked to the causes and consequences of war. They are, nevertheless, perpetuated as institutionalized and subtle destructive expressions of conflict even long after cessation of hostilities and signing of peace treaties. I illustrate below how the continuity of corruption, violence against women and attitudes towards diversity characterize areas as conflict-affected.

Countries that have transitioned into peacebuilding from war and armed conflict are ridden with bribery, fraud, conflicts of interest, nepotism and other forms of corruption. The 2015 Corruption Perception Index (Transparency International 2015) scores degrees of perceived corruption in the public sector of 168 countries from 0 to 100 (0 = highly corrupt). While the top ranks of Denmark (91) and Finland (90) show that no country is purely free of perceived acts of corruption, countries that have transitioned out of armed conflict in the past two decades float in the bottom half: Nepal (27), Lebanon (28), Guatemala (28), Sierra Leone (29), Kosovo (33), Sri Lanka (37), Bosnia and Herzegovina (38) and Rwanda (54). In Lebanon, the patriarchical engendering of political leadership (Joseph 1999a, b) and exclusive access to employment (Joseph 2005) are deep-rooted in nepotistic traditions that resemble pre-Islamic tribal organizations. Corruption has even damaged conditions for environmental sustainability. In Lebanon, mountains are mined by illegal quarries, waste is dumped into natural water resources, buildings are quickly constructed in urban green spaces and the government continues to struggle in resolving the garbage crisis following the closure of the overfilled main landfill in July 2015.

The ongoing structural and cultural violence against women is a global catastrophe and is exacerbated in areas that have passed through extreme violence. Women and children are among the most vulnerable during armed conflicts. Women raped during the genocide in Rwanda (Mukamana and Brysiewicz 2008) and widowed during the 2003–2008 Iraq war (Brand 2010) and civil war in Sri Lanka (Alwis 2002) struggle to raise children, find work, remarry and process war-related trauma because of cultural stigmas including having had a male partner. Lebanese women cannot pass on their Lebanese citizenship status to their children. This apparent violation of their children's rights to preserve their parent's national identity (Article 8, UNCRC) is deep-rooted in the power struggles between Muslims and Christians in Lebanon that has pushed Christian political leaders to heavily control the naturalization of Muslims. Despite Lebanon's standing as the most liberal and democratic member state of the Arab League, we still find the structural and cultural violence similar to the other member states that retain women as second-class citizens through the laws and socially constructed gender roles that dictate divorce, inheritance, mobility and protection.

Diversity is almost always associated with roots and expressions of destructive conflict. However, we must be clear that diversity is neither a form nor a root of conflict, but a condition or state of differences that is vulnerable to people's different and, sometimes, conflicting values and positions. Conflicts, whether as constructive or destructive expressions, result from the attitudes and actions towards these differences. Cultural diversity is no exception. The increase of cultural diversity in a single community can result from globalization (e.g. migration for economic opportunities), technology (e.g. ease of travel and shared platforms of communication) and war (e.g. forced displacement). As a result, variations of cultural variables like languages, religion, national identity, ethnicity, gender, race, [dis]abilities, sexual orientation and political parties increase. This growth of variations can generate creative and/or destructive tensions (Gutmann 2004), depending on the attitudes towards diversity. Vavrus (2012) illustrates conflicting perceptions of diversity according to a political economy spectrum of social conservatism, liberal multiculturalism and critical multiculturalism. Social conservatism – derived from principles of conservatism (cf. Burke and Scruton) – aims to safeguard traditional social structures, which means being extremely cautious towards, if not resisting, the Utopia of human rights. Liberalists like Kant set the foundations for liberal multiculturalism through an order of universalism that protects individual freedoms for equal opportunities and, as maintained by Kymlicka (1996), developing multicultural identities. While social conservatists find the variety of cultural expressions a threat to assimilation and liberal multiculturalists celebrate how communities comprising different cultures thrive together, critical multiculturalists aim to flatten hierarchies within multicultural communities by tackling roots to inequality and power struggles (Vavrus 2012). Within a context of diversity, tensions almost naturally arise when people – host, indigenous, migrants, refugees – are faced with cultural values and practices different from their own. What manifests tensions into structural and cultural violence is the absence of a shared vision and limited communicative capacities to ensure that these differences are constructive and sustainable and uphold the dignity of each individual.

Designing education as an intervention for development and social reconstruction in areas affected by or transitioning out of armed conflict is daunting. During war, school infrastructure is destroyed or transformed into prisons to accommodate systematic torture and executions. A damaged human capital includes a generation of children who have lost years of schooling and become orphaned, disabled or war veterans. Complicating matters even more, areas affected by conflict have culturally normalized forms of violence that sustain corruption; gender inequality; exclusive access to human rights of children, women and refugees; and unsustainable ways of managing the natural environment. In such a context, formal and non-formal education become critical approaches to peacebuilding to prevent re-escalation of armed conflict, transform conflict into constructive expressions and foster reconciliation among victims and perpetrators. Not any approach to designing and providing education, however, supports sustainable development and social reconstruction. In the remaining sections of this chapter, I outline the aims and negotiated positions of education for peacebuilding and their vulnerabilities to violence. This section provides the framework that I use to critically identify benefits as well as harms of citizenship education.

The faces of education for living together

Education research, design and provisions consistently appear in the front lines of post-armed conflict rhetoric. The reasons for turning to education are mostly incontestable. First and foremost, these sites are homes to tens of millions of children out of school. Access to quality education – safe, inclusive, collaborative and holistic – including resources and conditions is stipulated throughout the UN Convention on the Rights of the Child (UNCRC; United Nations 1989; see articles 19, 23, 24, 28, 29, 31–33, 40). The UNCRC is a legally binding instrument ratified by all countries but the United States of America. In 2012, 58 million children around the world aged 6 to 11 were reportedly out of school and 36 per cent of them live in countries affected by armed conflict (UNESCO 2015).

Educational programmes can provide school-aged children affected by armed conflict the necessary rehabilitation and support for healthy growth, social re-integration and academic achievement. When transitioning out of armed conflict, education can also provide the means and spaces for social reconstruction. In application, educational programmes would help reintegrate child soldiers into the community; ensure dismembered children have access to learning facilities; and gradually bring children from warring communities to learn together, from each other and about each other. Marginalized children would also attain literacy and vocational skills necessary for work opportunities that minimize chances of falling into poverty and strengthen economic growth. Education, therefore, becomes a lever for social justice. Quality learning programmes can also empower young people to live their young life as active citizens and be lifelong learners who can foster sustainably inclusive and equitable communities (Delors et al. 1996; Dewey 1944 [1916]).

The provisions of this children's human right, however, do not guarantee a safe, equitable, collaborative and dialogic learning environment for sustainable peace, justice and living. Education is influenced, designed and facilitated by individuals. Each of these individuals is defined by values, experiences, social constructs and personality traits shaped by genetic predispositions and upbringing. Education policies, practices and physical spaces are, therefore, extremely vulnerable to people's individual decisions, interpretations and culturally constructed environments. The outcomes can be detrimental to children's safety and human growth. Development education research (e.g. Bush and Saltarelli 2000; Gross and Davies 2015; Harber 2004; Smith and Vaux 2003; UNESCO 2011) reveals what Bush and Saltarelli (2000) describe as a second face to education that shows how classrooms, school play areas, curricula, instruction, testing, classroom management and even transportation to and from school can be sites of harm.

Harm in and through education can result from deprivation and direct violence. Deprivation includes the absence or removal of basic needs like nutrition, stable relationships, protection and any other basic need enshrined in the UNCRC. In instances of direct violence, harm is inflicted unto children like sexual abuse and harassment, forced recruitment into combat and corporal punishment. The contrasting forces of deprivation and direct violence often work in tandem. During armed conflict or war, schools become extremely vulnerable to violent attacks, especially when they lack virtually any protection from combat. On 6 December 2014, Taliban militia fighters massacred at least 132 children and 12 staff in a school in Peshawar, Pakistan. School children in countries still under armed conflict like Yemen, the Central African Republic, Afghanistan, Syria and Iraq live in daily uncertainty of falling victim to military strikes, soldier recruitment or schools transforming into prisons and military bases.

In this book, however, indications of benefits and harm are explored in practices and policies stemming from within the education system. Poor school infrastructure could deny children from accessing safe drinking water, clean bathrooms and even classrooms. Teachers who lack a written qualification to teach and opportunities for continuous professional development risk depriving children from receiving the necessary guidance when learning or managing emotions and relationships. In turn, their responses to children's learning and upbringing at school risk mirroring a teacher's authoritarian understandings and experiences of schooling. Structural violence can institutionalize deprivation when national policies prevent underrepresented people like girls, minority groups and refugees to attend schools as a mechanism to oppress these large populations. In some schools, children are not free from direct violence like murder, rape and corporal punishment. In April 2017, a Malaysian 11-year-old boy in a religious school in Singapore died in hospital after having both legs amputated from beatings with a water hose. With children's accessibility to mobile phones with cameras, incidents of principals and teachers physically beating school children are captured and posted online. Harber (2004) cites similar accounts in *Schooling as Violence*, showing school children as victims of murder, rape, corporal punishment and even systematic assessment.

The selection and delivery of curricular content have also made their way into the arsenal of warring parties. The selection of language can exclude or forcefully assimilate minority groups into the politically dominant culture (Churchill 1986). History education is another programme that officials control for political purposes. During times of ethnic conflict, history books are manipulated to reinforce stereotypes and prejudices (Bush and Saltarelli 2000). In Lebanon, confessional warring parties during the 15-year civil war wrote their own history books propagating their own heroes, victims and villains (Salibi 1988). Hence, the subsequent peace treat, the Ta'if Accord, called for a unified history book. Although the production of a grand narrative of history has mostly political aspirations of trying to foster social cohesion through nationalistic sentiment, the dogmatic texts and encouraged pedagogies of rote learning demonstrate an authoritarian ideology of a single, official story about the past (Seixas 2000). Indeed, the selection of historical events to produce a single narrative about the past means leaving some stories to be forgotten (Renan 1990); and these stories are mostly of minority and underrepresented groups. Moreover, requiring children to recite officiated information through systemic testing not only inflicts harmful levels of stress on the child's brain, but also denies them of any opportunity to think and argue critically.

Frameworks for examining education in conflict-affected areas

Numerous frameworks help us examine the extent to which education in areas affected by armed conflict supports the healthy growth of young people and empowers them to foster a socially cohesive and inclusive community (a vision of citizenship explored in Chapter 2). In a landmark UNESCO report, *Learning: The Treasure Within*, Delors et al. (1996) present four pillars of knowledge that enable young people to build socially cohesive communities. 'Learning to know' emphasizes the importance of learning how we learn – or metalearning – in order to improve how we learn and continuously construct and apply new knowledge as adults. By 'Learning to Be', young people develop a self-awareness of their personality traits, autonomy and responsibility. Under 'Learning to do', they work and learn together in different contexts; brainstorm, design and carry out projects; and produce creative expressions together. Through 'Learning to live together', learners put special emphasis on acknowledging and capitalizing on the diversity of ideas. They learn and work with people from different backgrounds on projects that address social injustices and manage conflict.

Children's human rights defined by the UNCRC has provided citizenship and human rights education research with another analytical framework. The UNCRC decrees the most basic standards of education for all children under 18. The intertwinement of ensuring that children have the unconditional right to education, learning about human rights and expressing their rights in and through education immediately positions young people into being active, engaged and empowered rather than as second-class citizens waiting to graduate to full citizenry (McCowan 2012; Osler 2016; Verhellen 2000). Tomaševski (2001) aligns the right to education and rights in and through education with a proposed framework of ensuring that education is available, accessible, acceptable and adaptable (four A's) when examining the obligations and capacities of government institutions in providing quality education for all. Osler (2016) couples Tomaševski's four A's with a children's human rights framework in an analysis of how human rights education is incorporated into learning, schooling and aims of education.

The right to access education, for example, is a critical starting point in exploring intersections of education in conflict-affected areas, citizenship and social cohesion. Following the genocide in Rwanda, the government used reforms to make sure that the Tutsi ethnic group who were marginalized by barriers to enter schools had the same access to schools as the Hutus in order to build a new culture of cohesion and social justice. In Lebanon, on the other hand, refugees from Palestine still cannot access public schools, although they can sit for the Lebanese Baccalaureate government exams following successful completion of years 9 and 12 in the UNRWA schools established for them. While the case in Rwanda attempts to deconstruct a history of marginalized citizenship of the Tutsis and, even prior, the Hutus, the exclusion of Palestinian refugees from state-funded schooling in Lebanon reinforces it. Even the arrangement of a second shift in Lebanese public schools set up only for refugee children from the war in Syria creates a complex construct of citizenship. Not only does the second shift build a segregated social structure between Lebanese and Syrian children, but also reinforces the second-class citizenry of Palestinian refugees over those from Syria and Iraq.

In this book, I mostly draw on the view of education as an approach to peacebuilding in areas affected by conflict to examine the extent to which citizenship education is beneficial, futile and harmful. Education for peacebuilding can be defined through three perspectives: education as a humanitarian response, education as conflict-sensitive and education for peacebuilding (Smith 2011, 2014; UNICEF 2011). Countries that have passed through long periods of swinging in and out of armed conflict (e.g. Sri Lanka, Lebanon, Palestine) demonstrate the complexities of simultaneously managing all three perspectives. In Lebanon, we recently saw an overlap as the need for humanitarian aid became vital for the sudden influx of over a million and a half refugees since the war erupted in Syria in 2011. Prior to the war in Syria, the Lebanese Ministry of Education and Higher Education (MEHE) and civil society organizations designed educational programmes after the 1975–1990 civil war to foster sustainable peace, empower young people as active democratic citizens and avoid any forms of conflict during schooling. Citizenship education through formal schooling is rarely provided in the form of humanitarian aid. This book zooms in on citizenship education through formal schooling, a provision in conflict-affected areas that we can examine through conflict-sensitive and peacebuilding perspectives.

Conflict-sensitive to 'do no harm'

From a conflict-sensitive perspective, education aims to avoid triggering or refuelling conflict by ensuring that learners neither address nor learn about information related to sources of conflict (Smith 2014). Areas affected by armed conflict rely a great deal on this approach when reforming education policy or facilitating new approaches to learning and teaching. The intention to avoid conflict in the classroom has shown to be beneficial when sensitivities to conflict were part of a wider activity on tackling sensitive or controversial issues. Learning history as a discipline is among the most conflict-charged fields of study in a national curriculum. Although learning about the 1975–1990 civil war is not part of the history national curriculum in Lebanon, the Lebanese Association for History (LAH) has developed over time a sequence of lessons to answer, 'Why did the civil war begin in 1975?' Before engaging history teachers in this extremely sensitive exercise, they first try to explain what broke the camel's back in Chapman's (2002) fictional story, 'Alfonse the Camel'. A main purpose of 'Alfonse the Camel' is to diagnose learners' levels of complexity when examining causes. Facilitators at LAH found this exercise invaluable because it gave the history teachers in Lebanon a dry run through the methods of using causation as a conceptual tool and, thus, helped maintain focus on the methodology as well as substantive knowledge.

The intention to 'do no harm' through classroom pedagogies can help create a safe environment for dialogues and debates over sensitive matters and conflicting ideas, values and knowledge. A safe classroom environment provides learners with a space to express their views without the fear of being hurt and without hurting others. University students from various religious sects in a summer school on peacebuilding and conflict transformation (Akar 2016) and history teachers in a professional development programme (Akar, Shuayb, and Hamadeh 2016) established class norms and had access to open writing spaces to help manage ideas and emotions during heated discussions. Establishing class norms that learners create together and keep accessible in the classroom provides a reference point to regulate dialogues when learners begin to feel frustrated, make logical fallacies and interrupt their peers. Also, learners extremely concerned with the ideas shared can get up at any time and write in spaces like a 'parking lot' or 'idea market', normally in the form of a white paper posted on the wall. How they are addressed or at least acknowledged later on depends on what the learners and teachers decide together. A safe learning environment also allows learners to manage negative feelings that can be triggered by addressing controversial issues. A civics teacher in Lebanon relied heavily on making time at the end of class for students to express their emotions in reflection journals. She believed that these reflection journals helped transform feelings of resentment and offence into safe and constructive learning experiences.

A conflict-sensitive perspective to school reform and classroom learning and teaching, however, can do more harm than good as a standalone approach. In some areas, education providers (i.e. government, private) have segregated children based on the cultural backgrounds that were regarded as sources of the armed conflict. This approach clearly undermines any greater aims and initiatives for post-armed conflict social cohesion. The 1992–1995 war in Bosnia and Herzegovina (BiH) cost the lives of over a quarter million people, mostly Bosnian Muslims (Bosniaks). After the war, the 'two schools under one roof' system aimed to provide schooling for children from various socio-ethnic identities and ensure they maintained their right to learn in their respective language (Bosnian, Croatian, Serbian) and study subjects like history and religion that emphasized ethnic-based values. The schools share the same campus but have different entrances and timetables to ensure that the students do not interact, for example during recess. This system aims to avoid generating new conflicts but clearly institutionalizes segregation. These schools still exist in some parts of BiH despite public outcry.

The curriculum is another component of education that is screened for associations with elements of a nation's violent past. During post-armed conflict education reform, policymakers normally demand a history curriculum that officiates only one narrative. The assumption behind this grand narrative approach to history education is that learning a single account of the past will not trigger debates but celebrate a common identity, heritage and set of victories to foster a sense of collective memory (Halbwachs 1950) and social cohesion (Seixas 2000). Writing a single historical narrative as official, however, is an illustration of an oxymoron, 'consensual history'. Besides promoting authoritarian-style pedagogies like memorization, approaches to writing a grand narrative has also resulted in gridlock of curricular reform. The history curriculum in Lebanon is the only programme of study that was not revised after the civil war. Historians representing various religious sects were called to write a consensual account of past events. However, objections to particular interpretations and inclusion/exclusion of certain content have put history education reform in stalemate after failed attempts in 1997, 2000 and 2012. Consequently, official exams still assess a history national curriculum last published in 1971.

The destructive outcomes of conflict-sensitive approaches are derived mostly from the assumption that the roots of conflict that should be avoided are forms of diversity, like diversity of interpretations of the past and diversity of confessional expressions. This is why governments of countries transitioning out of armed conflict embrace nationalist ideologies when rewriting education policy and aims of education. A national identity or discourse creates a community of sameness that has the power to bring people together (Anderson 1983) and strengthen solidarity (Miller 2000). However, when policymakers, teachers or principals avoid facilitating contexts where children from different backgrounds socialize, engage with different sources of information or discuss sensitive topics, they reinforce the social construction of diversity being a source of conflict. The fallacious reasoning that the state of diversity is a direct cause of destructive expressions of conflict overshadows any attention to the human error of lacking proficiency to manage emotions and dialogues when engaging with conflicting ideas, information and values. Education through a peacebuilding perspective aims to develop this proficiency so that people can think and behave critically with peers when exploring issues in their local and wider communities.

Peacebuilding and development

Times of social reconstruction and transformation also mean changes in ideologies and visions. Education becomes a critical opportunity for reviewing and developing the ideologies necessary for peacebuilding (Smith 2005). During such a period, education gives promise to new visions for sustainable living in diverse conflict-affected communities. Starkey (2012), for example, argues that the Universal Declaration of Human Rights provides a utopia of an unconditionally inclusive and just world order that education can aspire towards through dialogues on violations and celebrations of liberty and human dignity. Other visions of education are less encouraged. Delors (1996) urges to approach education not as a magical tool that completely rids society of injustices but, instead, as a tool to *'reduce* poverty, exclusion, ignorance, oppression and war' (13, emphasis by self). These two are rather contrasting approaches to reimagining aims of education for social reconstruction and peacebuilding. Nevertheless, they encourage young people to collaboratively and non-violently transform destructive expressions of conflict into constructive ones and explore how people from different cultural backgrounds can indeed live together.

How we conceptualize, institutionalize and utilize education will determine the extent to which transformations in conflict-affected areas ensure sustainable peace. Transformations influenced by education can be measured in areas affected by conflict by a 4R's framework: the reallocation of learning resources and access to learning (redistribution), importance given to diversity (recognition), inclusion of all education stakeholders in developing educational programmes (representation) and dialogues on roots and history of conflict (reconciliation) (Novelli, Lopes Cardozo, and Smith 2015). Although the framework does not make explicit mention of rehabilitating fighters, prisoners, the forcibly displaced and maimed people, any rehabilitative efforts would include reconciling with the victims, perpetrators and self in order to be recognized as an active citizen working towards sustainable peace. Educational programmes also result in intersections of these 4Rs. The initiative 'Fighters for Peace' (www.fightersforpeace.org) in Lebanon's civil society has brought together former fighters from the civil war to share with young people across the country their testimonies of the civil war and their personal transformations. This is one example of how education can redistribute information about a history of war, recognize the human dignity of individuals despite their violent past and make attempts to reconcile with warring parties by building new relationships through open dialogues.

Hence, the investment in citizenship education is a critical approach to peacebuilding. Citizenship education enables young people to capitalize from and celebrate diversity when fostering social cohesion and justice. It provides the necessary opportunities to manage the challenges of diversity and address injustices of political, social and economic systems. Through citizenship education, individuals learn to feel *unique as well as unified*. Whether as a single subject or whole-school approach, learning for citizenship at school creates a new social order governed by dialogue, mutual respect, collaboration and children's human rights. Formal and non-formal educational programmes that aim to foster these elements of active citizenship are still vulnerable to personality and individual differences. In 2010, an international agency commissioned me to develop an evidence-informed educational programme that promotes civic values and life skills. The final product, however, was shaped by a single person's vision of a pocket-size manual of content information for learners to know with no guidance on facilitating activities. At the government level, a director at the Lebanese MEHE expressed her scepticism towards student councils and, thus, scrapped the activity from a larger EU-funded support to citizenship education reform initiative. Even inside the classrooms, teachers may feel sensitive enough towards a topic and choose to avoid it completely. An awareness of conflict-sensitive approaches and negotiations with approaches to learning and teaching can minimize the threats of these vulnerabilities. A safe classroom environment is not meant to avoid conflict; instead, it prevents destructive expressions of conflict and transforms them into constructive ones. A recently published collection of testimonies from around world on good practices of teaching citizenship (Banks 2017) demonstrates how citizenship education can empower young people with approaches that enable them to learn and work with peers from different backgrounds, showing how they can capitalize on and celebrate diversity. Hence, activities designed to avoid conflict can truly empower learners as active citizens when it is a component of a larger scheme that capitalizes on conflict for long-term development like peacebuilding, social cohesion and active citizenship.

2

Constructing Ideals of Citizenship
for Living Together

In 2005, I visited Belfast to learn more about its sites of conflict and how citizenship was taught and learned in schools. I met with teachers, researchers and curriculum developers. After listening to their stories of breakthroughs and struggles, some insisted on giving me their personal tour of the city's Europa Hotel, cemeteries and roadside murals. I was taken aback to see the physical structures that bordered Catholic and Protestant communities from each other. A special moment took place while sitting on the grassy lawn of the Belfast City Hall. A small group of upper school-aged adolescents stopped to say hello and asked about my visit. Our conversation opened a discussion on citizenship. One described citizenship as going over and beyond of what is expected from our rights and responsibilities. I still reflect on this young person's insight, the motivations behind this idea and how it fits into the larger discourse of attempts to construct a normative ideal of citizenship. Defining an ideal construct of citizenship is the foundation for any design of citizenship education. It helps answer the question, 'Education for what *kind* of citizenship?' A defined ideal provides educationists with indicators to design, facilitate and assess learning. The young person's insight not only contributes to the diversity of citizenship ideals but underscores an element of agency that is commonly woven through visions of citizenship in areas affected by conflict.

This chapter defines a vision of citizenship for education in areas affected by armed conflict. It does not intend to construct a universal notion of citizenship for all times and cultures. Pocock (1995) and Heater (2004) contest such an attempt. The vision of citizenship in this discourse of education in conflict-affected areas responds to the demands of social reconstruction. An ideal citizenship also provides education researchers and practitioners with indicators for the design and evaluation of learning activities and programmes. To develop this vision or ideal, I first present citizenship in its most simple form: a relationship between individuals and communities. This relationship is composed of inter-related dimensions of status, feelings and practice that interplay across spectrums of active/passive or maximal/minimal notions of citizenship. I then contextualize active dynamics of citizenship within universal principles of living together, a vision of citizenship promoted in the highly influential UNESCO report, *Learning: The Treasure Within* (Delors et al. 1996). We also begin to see the cultural complexities of citizenship in Lebanon and the surrounding region through literature from the region on Islamic traditions, post-colonial Arab and Lebanese nationalisms, cosmopolitanism and human rights. The chapter concludes with a working definition of active citizenship for living together demonstrated by informed, engaged and empowered individuals.

The relationships between individuals and communities

We begin with the assumption that citizenship in the broadest sense is the relationship between individuals and their surrounding communities. Here, a community is a group or body that one is connected with. The idea that all human beings have some form of relationship with a community was once proclaimed by the English poet John Donne, 'No Man [*sic*] is an *Iland*, intire of it selfe' (1987 [1624], 87). A traditional understanding of one's community includes local social structures like a public library, municipality, police station, school, medical centre and place of worship.

We also have connections with other more abstract forms of communities. At a national level, the community can mean the nation-state or a pan-nationalistic identity like Arab, African, Pacific or European. Indeed, the political community associated with governance structures of the nation-state has constructed probably the most popular understanding of citizenship, if not the only one (e.g. Kivisto and Faist 2007; Walzer 1989). Within the spiritual community, one may share faith-based commitments with other worshippers while another might find solace among non-believers. At a global level, some people identify themselves with the human race and global movements that evolve from changes and discoveries about the world, including climate change, social justice and environmental sustainability. People may define their social and biological ecologies as communities, such as families, domestic animals and the natural environment and all its inhabitants. In today's digital age, the World Wide Web hosts platforms for social networking, sharing information, advocacy and trade – all of which constitute as communities that people interact through. The diversity of communities is further illustrated in the collection of chapters in the *Handbook of Citizenship Studies* (Isin and Turner 2002), which includes ecological citizenship, economic citizenship and sexual citizenship. Citizenship is therefore the constructed relationships within a multidimensional web of communities; this plurality has also been described as the community of communities (Parekh 2000) or multiple communities (Banks 2004b).

Elements of citizenship

The relationships between individuals and their communities are made up of elements. In the twenty-first century, citizenship scholars from disciplines like political science, history and education have deconstructed the concept of citizenship in order to define these elements. By identifying components of citizenship, we can review and develop proposed ideals (rhetoric) of citizenship, which provide an analytical framework to examine social/individual conceptualization (reality) and approaches to learning and teaching citizenship found in policy and pedagogy.

Isin and Turner (2002) describe citizenship as a 'language' of rights and obligations/duties (1). Turner (1997) argued that these rights and obligations determine one's legal status or formal identity and, consequently, entitlements to resources like social services, freedoms and cultural capital. They recognize the significance of T. H. Marshall's (1950) advocacy of social, political and civil rights as an impetus for advancing understandings of people's two-way relationship with society and the State (Isin and Turner 2007). They argue that this two-way relationship of rights and duties is constructed by three fundamental axes: extent, content and depth. The extent of citizenship refers to peripheries of participation like exclusion and inclusion. By examining content, we identify the particular 'benefits and burdens' defined through rights and obligations (Isin and Turner 2002, 4). Thirdly, the depth of citizenship shows the thickness and thinness of people's identities and other feelings of belonging and loyalty. Their understanding of citizenship is a bilateral relationship of rights (from State to people) and obligations (from people to State) constructed by these axes.

Another perspective identifies status, feelings and practice as elements that constitute citizenship, which Heater (2004) and Osler and Starkey (2005a) develop as a tripartite model of citizenship. While Heater (2004) contextualizes the model mostly for the political sphere, Osler and Starkey (2005a) explicitly define the three as inter-related dimensions of citizenship that provide the basis for a universal, cosmopolitan form of citizenship. Heater (2004), a historian of citizenship discourse, identified three components of citizenship to analyse traditions of citizenship. One component was 'feeling'. Feelings are observed as various forms of identities and emotional bonds like communalism, patriotism and sense of unity with all human beings. Our identities shape what we identify as civic virtues or moral responsibilities like integrity, community engagement and obligations. Heater identified people's behaviours in the political sphere as another component that defines citizenship. For example, the dominating political ideologies – from totalitarianism to liberal democracy to cosmopolitanism – and educational experiences largely influence why, how and how much people participate in public affairs. The third component of citizenship that Heater identifies is the civil and legal status of the individual. One's status as a migrant worker, refugee, tourist, naturalized citizen or national citizen through birth determines access to civil rights. Although Heater recognizes the world as a polity for human beings who have universal human rights, he deconstructs citizenship as the relationship people have with the political sphere.

What we see in common across most citizenship discourse that attempts to deconstruct the concept into foundational elements is a relationship based on rights and obligations determined by the legal or official status of the individual, which also shapes one's identities and degrees of participation. Osler and Starkey (2005a) bring these elements together into a holistic model of status, feelings and practice that allow us to examine the dynamic relationships within citizenship in a time of heightened globalization, migration and forced displacement. People's official or legal status defines their positions with the community. Citizenship with the nation-state consists of various types of legal status, such as citizens in the legal sense passed down from parent-holders or granted by the State after being born within its geographical territory. Some are naturalized after spending a certain amount of time or even capital inside that country. Others may have entered as migrants for work and study opportunities and, thus, granted visitor status. Among the most marginalized, however, are people who have been forcibly displaced from war and, thus, recognized as refugees or citizens-in-transit. These and nomadic or stateless but indigenous people have limited, if any, access to civil and human rights. Females and children are also vulnerable to legislature that ensures rights to and encourages participation from males and those over a defined age. Status determines one's civil, political and social rights and obligations which help us understand the struggles and challenges of migrants and refugees actively participating in society. Indeed, the nature of human rights provides all whose status is 'human being' an unconditional right to dignified living set out in the UN Declaration of

Human Rights; legally binding instruments, or conventions, have been ratified for children (UNCRC) and women (CEDAW).

The second element features feelings of identity, belonging, inclusion or exclusion, nationalism and fairness. The status that is granted can influence how close, loyal or committed one feels towards that community or its people. Tourists and others visiting a different country for short-stay purposes like students in an exchange programme may not feel as isolated as refugees or migrants whose legal status denies them from access to virtually all civil rights in that country. In tandem, this affective dimension influences our behaviours and, to an extent, vice versa. Practice is the third element that includes behaviours like voting, recycling, protesting, defending the rights of others and even showing integrity. Deconstructions of citizenship reveal these three recurring elements, which have survived social and political changes throughout history.

Spectrums of citizenship

The extent to which we feel we belong [and to where] or are empowered can determine how we approach municipalities, engage in dialogues and dispose of our garbage. These dynamics result from the degrees of feelings and participation in the inter-relationships of status, feelings and practice. Spectrums illustrating behaviours and feelings of citizenship have mostly developed through discourse on democratic citizenship. McLaughlin (1992) proposes that we view these degrees through understandings of maximal and minimal notions of citizenship. For the pluralistic democratic society, he illustrates these notions in an exercise describing degrees of identity, virtues, political involvement and social presuppositions. A minimal notion of citizenship limits the scope of identity to a legal status defined by the nation-state and narrows participation to the local area and law-abiding actions. On the other hand, a maximal notion of citizenship is more open to encompass the public sphere and other communities (e.g. regional, global, human, environmental). It constructs various identities and engagement is based on exercising freedoms, critical thought and active participation.

Active and passive forms of citizenship provide another spectrum of participation and feelings that define various degrees of agency. The active citizen is an agent of change who is *informed* of obligations, civil and human rights and topical issues; *empowered* by literacy, ability to mobilize and access to platforms; and *engaged* in critical discourse, advocacy and proactive initiatives. These facets that define a spectrum of agency are found in other models of citizenship that outline attributes of active/passive citizens. They do not directly resemble the typical classification of knowledge, skills, attitudes, values and sometimes identity that we see in models of democratic citizenship like the civic competence inventory (Hoskins 2013), enlightened political engagement (Parker 2004) and active citizenship for democracy (Abs and Veldhuis 2006). Nevertheless, the degrees of empowerment and engagement and how much one is informed make up the citizenship knowledge largely constituted of the amalgamation of knowledge, skills, attitudes and values.

The specific features of this definition are outlined in a framework of indicators of civic competence for active democratic citizenship – knowledge, skills, attitudes, values and identities (Hoskins et al. 2008).[1] The knowledge component informs people of their rights, heritage and current events. The culmination of skills (e.g. conflict resolution, critical analysis, advocacy, collaboration) with attitudes (e.g. feeling confident and open to differences) and knowledge determines degrees of empowerment for participation. How and where they engage also depend on the overlaps of all four features. Human rights, democracy and values like respect for differences provide overarching principles, which I discuss as an overarching framework in the next section.

Moving away from the 'active' and towards the 'passive' end of the spectrum, the degrees of agency begin to change. Rather than proactively engaging in movements, citizens in this middle sphere of participation mostly react to one-off activities, like joining a protest or signing a petition to show solidarity. They participate mostly by abiding by the laws. Closer to the passive end of the spectrum, individuals become less informed about their rights and obligations; disempowered by illiteracy or status; and not engaged in public discourse, the community or activities for development and sustainability.

In citizenship studies, researchers have referred to passive forms of citizenship as inactive (Hoskins et al. 2012) and silent (Gest and Gray 2015) when investigating why people exhibit low degrees of participation and agency. One reason is that some conceptualize the notion of a good citizen as a law-abiding member of the community and, thus, choose not to engage in activities that potentially lead to change. Another reason for low- or no-impact participation is the lack of feeling motivated and finding no interest or benefit from active engagement; hence, they choose to opt out. A third reason is when

---

[1] The indicators of civic competencies for promoting active democratic citizenship were drawn from European Union legislation (European Parliament and Council 2006) and the European Commission's Centre for Research on Education and Lifelong Learning.

people are marginalized or disenfranchised from accessing participation spaces and developing tools like literacy because of their legal status (e.g. nationality, age, gender) or race. Banks (2015) coins this intentional neglect to empower minority, vulnerable and underrepresented groups as failed citizenship. In turn, people of failed citizenship can detach themselves from even the most basic of social services. In 2015, I sat with a Syrian refugee father in a tent in West Bekaa, Lebanon, because we learned that he refused to send his children to school despite access to provisions of state education by the Lebanese government. He believed that his dignity as a human being was violated along with all his human rights by the Lebanese government. He described a broken and abusive unilateral relationship between his family and the host government. Therefore, he did not see how he or his family could engage in any of the government's institutions, even schools, and chose to protest and safeguard whatever humanness he still felt inside.

Neither inactive, silent nor passive citizens cause harm as they try to fulfil their most basic of obligations like stopping at a red light and placing rubbish in the bin. However, the passive citizen can become 'merely a subject of an absolute authority' (Turner 1990, 209). Passivity, however, towards injustices normalized through structural violence could reinforce powers that maintain the marginalization of vulnerable groups. With time, communities implode when rising against oppression and create political vacuums that are often quickly seized by fundamentalist groups. In the Arab region, the second decade of the twenty-first century witnessed waves of violent and non-violent uprisings against oppressive regimes. The people's passivity had created and sustained a degree of habituation or normalcy over generations to the oppression and marginalization of dictatorial governance, like those in Tunisia, Libya, Egypt and Yemen.

Certain forms of participation have been debated as either active or passive. In an exercise where university students in Lebanon ordered attributes of a 'good citizen' on a range of passive to active, many debated over voting as an active or passive expression of citizenship. They described voting as passive when it is expected by family members or partisans of a political party to unconditionally and uncritically vote for their party's leader. Others argued that voting is active when the choice to elect a candidate is driven by a sound manifesto or protest towards other candidates. Debates have also challenged the moral judgement of those who choose not to engage. Van der Ploeg and Guérin (2016) challenge the apparent stigma associated with non-participation. They draw on Brennan's (2011) argument that democracy can survive and indeed flourish when a population of citizens choose not to participate in the political sphere; the private sphere like running a business, raising children or working as a janitor can also exercise civic virtues in a liberal society.

The degrees of agency illustrated in a passive/active spectrum often evolve as responses to perceived stability of a government. In the cases of Cyprus and Greece, Hoskins et al. (2008) interpreted their high levels of participatory attitudes compared to most of Europe as a reaction to their unstable democracies. However, most migrants forcibly displaced by armed conflict have limited access to civil and even human rights because of their legal status as refugees. Consequently, they are more likely to live as subjects or citizens-in-transit in the host country. Indeed, some prefer to maintain a low profile. Many refugees in Lebanon from Syria – especially males eligible for serving the Syrian military – feared persecution from their government and, so, avoided even registering at the UNHCR.

Principles of citizenship for living together

Unlike the three dimensions of citizenship (status, feelings and practice), the forms of participation that fall along active/passive or maximal/minimal spectrums of agency are defined by the principles of an envisioned citizenship. Under dictatorial rule, the spectrum of citizenship follows principles of authoritarianism and fundamentalism. An active form of authoritarian citizenship may be demonstrated by a selected elite who maintain order through oppression while passive forms of citizenship include unconditional compliance, which would be equally desirable by the governing dictatorship. Active citizenship based on democratic and human rights principles can benefit others and the State as opposed to interests of a certain party or self (Janoski and Gran 2002) and promote inclusion in societies diversified by religious and ethnic communities (Kiwan 2008). Without an explicit declaration of principles, the interpretations of participation (from active to passive) risk justifying various forms of destructive and oppressive actions.

Defining principles of citizenship is dynamic; its constructions are triggered and shaped by discoveries, injustices and changes. Change is an inherent attribute to the cultural context of any community, whether the nation, nation-state, region or world. In the twenty-first century, some of the most notable changes include mass migrations of forcibly displaced people from war, overthrows of long-reigning dictators, growing evidence of climate change and direct violence towards women sustained by male-dominated cultural norms. To overcome developmental tensions and reduce social injustices, the landmark Delors report, *Learning: The Treasure Within*, coins a vision of learning to live together (Delors et al. 1996). Delors (1996) maintains that living together in diversity and conflict is realized through democratic principles and personal and social development by, for example:

- having a sense of responsibility to participate in the public sphere,
- exercising emotional intelligence when adapting to change and demonstrating creative potentials,
- gaining the necessary knowledge to innovatively solve problems and create opportunities and
- working on understanding people who may appear different or even a threat.

Drawing on similar principles of active participation and learning about people from other cultures, authorities in citizenship education like Banks et al. (2005) and Osler and Starkey (2005a) have contextualized their compelling calls for a renewed vision of citizenship for a world that is increasingly diverse and vulnerable to violations of human rights. Their advocacy for, respectively, multicultural citizenship and cosmopolitan citizenship comes largely as a response to the dangers of a sole or narrow commitment to nationalism.

Nationalist discourse makes a 'sharp distinction between national citizens and foreigners' (Osler and Starkey 2005a, 20), which creates a pretext for discrimination and even armed conflicts. Guibernau (2007) acknowledges positive aspects of nationalism but cautions of racism and social exclusion as its 'dark side' since it can also be 'associated with those who advocate xenophobia and ethnic cleansing' (177). A dominant culture of national sentiments can generate an us-versus-them discourse that sets the groundwork for racial discrimination (Edwards 2009). Even in citizenship education (Akar and Albrecht 2017), language learning (Churchill 1986) and history education (Renan 1990; Seixas 2000), the uncritical building of a national consciousness can undermine educational aims for inclusion, social justice and critical pedagogies.

The dark side of nationalism finds cultural identities that differ from the nationalist attributes threats to prosperity, social justice and dignity. It harbours populism, fascism and racism and manifests into xenophobic and populist discourse and violence like ethnic cleansing and genocides. The destruction and atrocities to human lives from the two world wars gave a new momentum to Immanuel Kant's vision of humanity as a universal polity. In 1948, the UN General Assembly adopted the Universal Declaration of Human Rights (UDHR), an instrument that upholds the entitlement to dignity and freedoms of every human being. It also set the foundation for subsequent conventions that ruled entitlements specific to vulnerable populations, namely women (Convention on the Elimination of All Forms of Violence Against Women 1979) and children (Convention on the Rights of the Child 1989). These human rights instruments help construct a global world order that gives shape to cosmopolitanism as a philosophy (Nussbaum 1997) and utopia (Starkey 2012) where a community of humanity sets a minimum standard of living for all human beings to be compatible with all social and political ideologies. They also require a form of citizenship that champions intercultural communications (Osler and Starkey 2015) and reflections of multiple identities (Osler and Starkey 2005a). Cosmopolitanism and the human rights principles it upholds share and even reinforce principles found in nation-states' constitutional and political discourses (Goodman 2007; Tan 2010).

A citizenship for sustainable peace and justice draws on human rights and democratic principles. These principles underpin a citizenship essential for areas emerging out of armed conflict, struggling with structural violence and addressing social injustices. Social and political scientists have adopted some of these core principles as civic virtues (Kymlicka 2001; e.g. civility, sense of solidarity, respect others' rights), procedural values (Parekh 2000; e.g. tolerance, dialogue and mutual respect) and presuppositions (Crick 2000; e.g. respect for reasoning and fairness). We can also draw on the set of four principles and ten concepts that a consensus panel chaired by James Banks published for democratic nation-states living in a world dominated by nationalist rhetoric and vulnerable to injustices from globalization. Banks et al. (2005) proclaim that citizenship in an increasingly diverse and globalized world requires people to reflect on (1) the relationships between diversity and unity, (2) how all people are interconnected and interdependent, (3) human rights as a standard and ethical framework and (4) experience and participation to deliberate young people as citizens-in-waiting so they live as active citizens in school.

Citizenship for living together, especially in areas affected by armed conflict, demand the intersections of principles of human rights, understanding differences and active participation. These allow people to capitalize on the consolidations of cosmopolitanism and nationalist ideologies to feel *unique and unified* by reflecting on their multiple identities, managing emotions, enquiring to learn about differences and creating solidarity when addressing social injustices. Principles and values that underpin a notion of active citizenship must, nevertheless, be considered from within the cultural context of the area examined, in this case, Lebanon and the wider region. This exploration of discourse acknowledges and reveals diverse, conflicting and shared principles for living together sustainably.

Contextualizing citizenship through literature discourse

On 8 October 2017, the Lebanese Minister of Foreign Affairs, Gebran Bassil, tweeted in Arabic: 'Racist in our Lebaneseness, Oriental in our composition and international in our diaspora.' The message not only celebrates a cosmopolitan view of Lebanese nationalism, but encapsulates the general climate of resistance to the settlement of refugees from Syria, Palestine and Iraq in Lebanon. Over 1.5 million forcibly displaced people from the war in Syria have taken refuge in Lebanon, a country of 4 million people. In addition to distress over limited resources, people and confessional groups of Christian identity have voiced anxieties concerning the rise of a Muslim population. In a BBC HARDtalk interview[2] on 16 March 2016, the former Minister of Education Elias Bou Saab explicitly defended the importance of limiting refugees' civil rights to minimize a growth in the Muslim community, which threatens the positional powers of minority Christian groups. However, these messages reveal even a more discerning matter: conservative nationalist rhetoric that reinforces constructs of racism and xenophobia are normalized and to the extent that the high-ranking government officials assume the Lebanese and international communities will endorse. This dark side of nationalist discourse has also manifested into a Lebanese citizenship education curriculum that promotes social exclusion and limits critical and dialogic pedagogies (Akar and Albrecht 2017).

The wider region of West Asia and North Africa comprises multifaceted and complex constructs of citizenship. Deconstructing definitions and elements of citizenship from its literature discourse helps identify the communities that its people engage with and related tensions and opportunities in order to scaffold an ideal notion of citizenship. In Arabic, the primary language used across the entire region, two words directly translate into citizenship: *jinsiyyah* as one's national legal status and *muwātanah* – derived from *watan* or nation – for feelings and practices associated with a country. However, scholarship from the region in

---

[2]   http://www.bbc.co.uk/programmes/p03lyvf3

history and philosophy suggests that early constructs of citizenship developed towards communities of kin or tribal relations, religion and its doctrines and then extended towards national polities (Parolin 2009). Indeed, the phrase that Islam is *dīn wa-dawla*, or religion and the State (cf. Khalidi 1992), illustrates the basis of religion in, for example, political models of citizenship. Classical literature between the tenth and fourteenth centuries by al-Ghazāli and Ibn Khaldūn provide a pathway that reveals the historical significance of religion and social organizations as core elements of citizenship in WANA prior to the rise of nationalisms.

Islam, a core sphere

Al-Ghazālī (d.1111) was a Persian theologian who later became an *imām*, a religious authority, and later referred to as *hujjat al-ilsām*, or proof of Islam. After studying the Greek philosophers, al-Ghazālī rejected occidental philosophy since logic failed at producing truth or certainty when dealing with religious questions (Campanini 1996). Still valuing logical reasoning on a theological framework, he founded a tradition that sees Islam as the only means to living life on Earth. Citizenship, therefore, was solely of a spiritual-based nature. According to al-Ghazālī, the individual participates in two relationships: with other Muslims and with non-Muslims. Only Muslims and the Jewish and Christian communities they had positive relations with – and indeed only men – participated in the *umma* or the public sphere or community. Thus, Al-Ghazālī (1980 [1097]) described the relationship between two Muslims as a brotherhood and further parallels it to the contracts of marriage. As for the non-believers of one God, he regarded them as sinners or *kāfirūn* who lost all rights and privileges and possibly even their life (Al-Ghazālī 1980). This early scholarship during the eighth to twelfth centuries AD conceptualized a citizenship whereby religious dogma established the principles that would govern how and how much people could participate in all other spheres. Religion-based citizenship continues in modern times, but with interpretations that form extremist and discriminatory views to more liberal orientations advocating for sustainable peace and living in multicultural communities.

Social organizations for survival

Ibn Khaldūn (2005 [1370]), a historian, anthropologist and philosopher during the fourteenth century, described the *umma* as a tribe that maintains the traditions of Islam and where people's survival depended on its social and political dynamics. Attributing human beings with the ability to think critically, Ibn Khaldūn observed how people realized they could only survive through social organizations where people could collaborate with each other and exercise mutual respect. He also found that social groups strengthened fighting capabilities for tribal wars and the mutual affection among tribesmen strengthened their trust and commitments to each other. Social organizations such as tribes and allies with other Muslims ensured survival. Some Jewish and Christian groups were still connected with them as 'protected groups' (Watt 1979, 75). Ibn Khaldūn also learned that humans by nature socialized and formed relationships despite differences and associations with common origins such as family-generated stronger group feelings. Moreover, common descent shows greater mutual affection, support and aid, which enemies feared; hence, when forming tribal coalitions, those who valued family relationships were considered allies for survival.

Communitarian feelings were so essential for survival that Ibn Khaldūn measured the quality of a social organization through *asabiyyah* or the feeling of solidarity. Without family or close kin to care for, individuals cannot feel close to others and thus 'cannot live in the desert' because they will 'fall prey to any nation' (Ibn Khaldūn 2005 [1370], 98). Communities of people with common descent and close relations with allies, clients and neighbours were, therefore, far superior to those composed of many different groups whose diversity made them prone to tensions, conflicts and weak group structures (Ibn Khaldūn 2005 [1370]). He believed that people in diverse communities were more politically driven, seeking power and control while blood relatives protected each other to avoid feelings of shame when close contacts are treated unjustly or humiliated. In modern times, however, citizenship research has shown how communitarianism (Beiner 1995) and kinship (Joseph 1999a) can undermine fairness and codes of ethics through a culture of nepotism.

Once the tribespeople would form their groups or communities, human nature would at some point take its course again with individuals and leaders instinctively seeking greater power, even if through hostilities, aggression, corruption and ruthlessness (Ibn Khaldūn 2005 [1370]). The successful and great leaders, according to Ibn Khaldūn, facilitated democratic living through political and religious laws and consensus. The life of the social organization depended on consensual agreements. The people would appoint a leader, such as an *imām*, who would facilitate consensus to preserve religion and governance. Religious laws legislated everyday values for living and enjoying the afterlife while political laws, based on the framework of religious doctrines, would 'concern only worldly interests' (Ibn Khaldūn 2005 [1370], 155). Not only did Ibn Khaldūn distinguish between the religious and political spheres, but he also introduced a sense of cosmopolitanism, an awareness to the world community. Clearly, the governance of social organizations valued democratic procedures and principles which included the appointment of leaders and consensual agreements so long as they adhered to Islamic doctrine.

Nationalisms and cosmopolitanism

In addition to kinship and religion, orientations of citizenship across WANA were further developed through nationalisms and elements of cosmopolitanism. The region comprises a rich diversity of nationalistic ideologies including those particular for a nation-state, an imagined nation-state like Greater Syria and a supranational pan-Arab nation. During Ottoman rule, Arab nationalism transpired as an intellectual discourse to preserve the Arabic language and create a sense of solidarity among the Arab nations (Hourani 1991).

Arab nationalism re-emerged in the twentieth century in many forms. During Lebanon's mandate under French rule (1920/1923–1943), Antoun Saadeh opposed colonial governance through a discourse of Syrian nationalism. In 1932, he founded the secular Syrian Socialist Nationalist Party (SSNP) to unify countries neighbouring Lebanon into a single nation, Greater Syria. The SSNP is still active in 2017 as an ally of Hezbollah in the war in Syria and facilitator of summer camps for youth across Lebanon (Albrecht and Akar 2016). Later in the 1960s, pan-Arabism became a platform for Gamal Abdel Nasser in Egypt when calling for Arab nationalism to create solidarity among the Arab nations to protest Israel's occupation of Palestine. Abdel Nasser's pan-Arab vision, however, failed when he stretched it beyond its ideological limitations by attempting to unify neighbouring countries into a single Arab nation-state (Frisch 2001; Tibi 1997). While Arab nationalism maintained a socially constructed Muslim identity, the advocacy for Syrian nationalism was made through secular ideologies.

Nationalist discourses strengthened across WANA during the dissolution of French and British governance (Akar and Ghosn-Chelala 2015; Frisch 2001). For the new nation-states, they aimed to preserve heritage, foster a common unifying identity through a national consciousness and demonstrate sovereignty and intellectual autonomy. In Lebanon, negotiating the ideologies of Arab and Lebanese nationalisms, however, became a challenge. During the mandate, Lebanese Christian groups and their French allies constructed a nationalistic rhetoric of Phoenician roots to the Lebanese identity, which challenged the significance of the Arab cultural heritage (Firro 2004; Kaufman 2001). These competing Arab and Lebanese nationalist discourses have maintained the roots of many armed conflicts in Lebanon.

While nationalist movements spread as a modern phenomenon, cosmopolitanism survived centuries of competing political ideologies. Cosmopolitanism can be traced back to the Stoics in the third century as a polity of humankind. In the eighteenth century, Immanuel Kant developed this ideology into a universal order of moral principles for living together that later defined the notion of cosmopolitan citizenship. During the European Enlightenment, Kant (2006 [1795]) maintained that, by nature, human beings remain in a state of war and, thus, peace would require a universal order of rights rather than agreements between nations. And while supporting the sovereignty of nation-states, Kant (2006 [1795]) called for 'a federation of peoples' with a higher law of international human rights (78). Kant's doctrines influenced the establishments of institutions like the League of Nations and the United Nations (Kleingeld 2006). The United Nations and its agencies championed the writing of human rights instruments (e.g. UDHR, UNCRC, CEDAW). Cosmopolitan citizenship relies on human rights instruments to illustrate and set out the fundamental principles of its liberal philosophy that uphold the dignity and freedoms of all human beings who, by birthright, are citizens of the world (Nussbaum 1997; Starkey 2012). Traditionalists in citizenship discourse who reject the model of a cosmopolitan citizenship believe that rights and responsibilities can only be legislated and governed by a State, not a supranational polity (Linklater 2002) like humanity or the world. In the twenty-first century, however, the polity of humankind has become a new world public sphere realized through technology (Habermas 1995). Affordable travel, social media platforms, world news applications and online crowdfunding have informed, engaged and empowered people into active world citizens showing how the polity of humanity is indeed real and in effect.

In WANA, elements of cosmopolitan principles like universalism were present in various degrees through supranational communities like pan-Arabia and Islam and sub-national communities like a tribe or family (Dannreuther 1999). Looking beyond national political borders allowed for a global hybrid of cultural activities demonstrating how nations can capitalize on the diversity of knowledge, art and other cultural works from around the world. This multicultural dimension to cosmopolitanism thrived in WANA between the eighth and fifteenth centuries through al-Andalus (Arab Spain), the translation of Aristotle's works into Arabic before English and its incorporations into Islamic scholars' sciences, and, during the Ottoman empire, Namik Kemal who 'translated Montesquieu, debated Voltaire and Condorcet' and tried to express ideas of the Enlightenment using Islamic idioms (Zubaida 2002, 34). However, British and French rule in the region prior to and following the First World War tainted the construct of a cosmopolitan mindset. Albeit the colonial influence that Europeanized culture in places like Egypt gave rise to a 'golden age of Middle Eastern cosmopolitanism', the religious and nationalist movements like the Muslim Brotherhood in Egypt and Arab films and literature flourished to eradicate European imperial influence that conflicted with pan-national values (Zubaida 2002, 38). The traditions of enriching knowledge production and art by learning about cultures outside the region were overpowered by nationalistic movements that countered cultural influence from imperial rule. Other tensions in orientations of cosmopolitanism emerged when negotiating universal notions like human rights.

A range of political figures and movements across WANA have advocated for and endorsed a universal world order of entitlement to human rights. Charles Malik, a Lebanese philosopher, politician and diplomat, played a significant role in the leadership of designing and securing consensus of the UDHR. Despite resistances from communist nations and extreme liberal ideologists, Malik secured unanimous approval when he justified universal claims for the individual who is 'uniquely valuable to himself, but as constituted in part by and through his relationships with others – his family, his community, his nation, and his God' (Glendon 2000, 3). Charles Malik was an active cosmopolitan citizen through his advocacy work for a world order based on core freedoms that all human beings are entitled to.

The development of human rights instruments in WANA demonstrated governments' and civil societies' commitments to protecting vulnerable people against political and social oppression, censorship and assassinations of journalists, denial of women's rights and the torture and execution of prisoners in the region. These instruments include the Arab Human Rights Charter (1994); the Casablanca Declaration of the Arab Human Rights Movement (1999); the Cairo Declaration on Human Rights Education and Dissemination (2000); the Beirut Declaration: Toward an Effective Regional Protection of Human Rights (2003); and the Sana'a Declaration on Democracy, Human Rights and the Role of the International Criminal Court (2004). It did, however, take a few decades after the UDHR for the Arab League to establish a human rights committee for the region following pressure from the international community and a Year of Human Rights programme in 1966. In 1983, the Arab Organization for Human Rights was founded as an NGO followed by similar country-specific establishments across the region (e.g. Egyptian Organisation for Human Rights, Palestinian Organisation for Human Rights, Tunisian Human Rights League and the Lebanese Center for Human Rights). The slow and partial responses from the Arab countries to establish a human rights committee and charter and the loopholes in the Arab Human Rights Charter (1994) and nation-states' constitutions that undermine human rights reflected 'total neglect' and a 'negative climate' towards an ethos of human rights (Ghalyoun 2009, 346). The Casablanca Declaration of the Arab Human Rights Movement, for example, tried to reconcile human rights with Arab and Islamic culture by illustrating their overlaps. Also, in critical response to the Arab Human Rights Charter (1994) that appeared to undermine key human rights principles, the Beirut Declaration in 2003 aimed at modifying the charter to better reflect the core principles of the UDHR across the region (Chase and Hamzawy 2006).

A majority of nations throughout the WANA region, however, have expressed reservations to human rights discourse and instruments on grounds of religious doctrine (e.g. Shari'a law) and political positions (e.g. occupation of Palestine). In producing a human rights instrument that upholds pan-nationalist ideologies, the Arab Charter on Human Rights was adopted on 15 September 1994; by 2017, 17 out of the 22 Arab League member states had endorsed it and 14 had ratified it. In the English translation (Al-Midani and Cabanettes 2006), its preamble reaffirms the principles of the UDHR, including the basic 'right to a life of dignity based on freedom, justice and peace' and equal treatment regardless of any differences (150). At the same time, it promulgates its cultural traditions and principles by specifically rejecting Zionism (Preamble) and stating conditions for the death penalty (articles 10, 11 and 12). In addition, over half the twenty-two Arab nations stated their commitments to the treaties insofar as they did not conflict with the principles, provisions and precepts of the Islamic law, otherwise known as Shari'a (cf. Chase and Ballard 2006). This condition is controversial for two main reasons. First, making special provisions for people, such as those convicted of crimes and sentenced to death, sets a precedent that gives certain people less-than-human attributes and, consequently, undermines the dignity of being human. We also see this in article 3, which unintentionally reinforces structural violence against women: 'Men and women are equal in respect of human dignity, rights and obligations within the framework of the positive discrimination established in favour of women by the Islamic Shari'a, other divine laws and by applicable laws and legal instruments' (Al-Midani and Cabanettes 2006, 151). Despite the explicit intention to commit to the dignity and social justices of women, the writing of laws based on 'positive discrimination established in favour of women' safeguards men's interpretations of what is in the best interest of women that are decreed into religious and civil laws.

Second, they suggest that the interpretation of religious doctrine is fixed. However, one Islamic scholar and political activist from Sudan in the mid-twentieth century dedicated his life to show how entitlements to human rights and the core ideologies of Arabism and Islam can indeed support each other. Mahmoud Mouhamad Taha argued that Shari'a Law was based on selected verses from the Holy Qur'ān to serve a particular point in time and, in the twentieth century, impede any attempts to ensure full entitlements of human rights to all human beings (Hamad 2009). He, therefore, advocated for a revision of Shari'a Law based on principles of co-existence, empowerment of women and freedom enshrined in many of the holy scripture's abrogated verses. The Sudanese government charged Mahmoud Taha with apostasy and sedition and sentenced him to death; he died of hanging on 18 January 1985. I clearly do not suggest that Shari'a Law be revised; I only introduce the notion that universalistic principles of equality, freedom and human rights are common to cosmopolitanism and Islam. The same perspective follows for cosmopolitanism and nationalist ideologies.

Juxtaposing cosmopolitanism and nationalism to illustrate conflicting discourses is not only 'cliché' (Kymlicka 2001, 204), but also misleading. Promoting sentiments for the nation-state may appear under threat when situating the public sphere within a polity of humanity. However, the principles argued for both polities include freedom, mutual respect, active participation, inclusion and other humanistic and democratic principles. The national identity that policymakers hope will create a sense of unity or solidarity following armed conflict is actually a universal entitlement to an identity and national belonging. Also, the threats of diversity (multiple identities, migrants, etc.) expressed in nationalistic discourse can be controlled, minimized and even transformed to create constructive relationships under a human rights dimension. Elements of a humanistic framework facilitate the same mediators that, according to intergroup contact theory (a field of study in social psychology), minimize prejudice (Allport 1954), reduce anxieties (Blascovich et al. 2001) and enhance empathy, intergroup trust and perspective-taking (Pettigrew and Tropp 2011). For example, a cosmopolitan notion of citizenship establishes an equal status (being human), helps identify common struggles and encourages work towards a common goal. The processes of intergroup contacts can also help clarify misunderstandings and facilitate opportunities for collaboration and interaction through dialogues.

As ever, the need to at least explicitly recognize the reciprocity between cosmopolitanism and nationalism is critical for constructing an ideal vision of citizenship, especially in areas affected by conflict. As levels of diversity increase and demands to address corruption, reintegrate child soldiers and engage in dialogues about a violent past become so dire, the image of the 'good citizen' comprises attributes far beyond the symbolic attachments to one's nation-state. Mastering more than one language, preparing for the global labour market and learning about issues that affect people around the world, for example, have already made their way to a construct of an ideal national citizen. Each nation-state still has a great deal of room to 'reimagine the nation as cosmopolitan' (Osler 2010, 221), which will in turn further empower, engage and inform young people as active citizens.

Active citizenship for living together

Active citizenship for a democratic society has been commonly defined as 'participation in civil society, community and/or political life, characterized by mutual respect and non-violence in accordance with human rights and democracy' (Hoskins 2006, 6). I draw on this model and expand it to create a spectrum showing degrees of agency, particularly for areas affected by conflict. Hence, I conclude this chapter by forging principles of citizenship recognized as critical for post-conflict social reconstruction with facets of active citizenship that envision a citizen for living together in sustainable peace. States affected by armed conflict and that continuously struggle with other destructive expressions of violence including corruption, discrimination and exclusive participation have in many forms subscribed to principles of human rights, democratic participation, social justice, open dialogues and intercultural living. They commonly strive, in rhetoric at least, for national reconciliation, transforming conflict, fostering social cohesion, empowering young people to dialogue with peers from different cultural backgrounds, raising public awareness, advocacy and building sustainable relationships. The ideal citizen for these aims of social reconstruction, therefore, needs to be informed, engaged and empowered to uphold the principles listed above.

An active citizen for living together in areas affected by conflict is *informed* about current events and topical issues taking place across various communities that show social injustices, ongoing conflicts and even movements for positive change. This also includes knowledge about concepts and possible tensions or conflicts in their definitions. Practices of corruption in one culture, for instance, may seem acceptable in another, like giving a present to a teacher. The notion of peacebuilding in Lebanon has received much resistance from members of government agencies and the community because of the inference of making peace with Israel, an extremely controversial notion with legal implications. Active citizens are also informed of procedures and processes of engagement from knowing how to apply for a passport or national identification card to registering a non-governmental organization or filing a civil complaint. Finally, active citizens know their civil and human rights and what national, regional and international governance systems expect from them.

Empowerment enables people to take action. Active citizens are *empowered* through literacies that enable them to think critically, access and read information and engage in critical yet rational discourse. In other words, empowered democratic and world citizens know how to access and use the knowledge or information available. In an oversimplification of Habermas's (1984 [1981]) theory of communicative action, the pragmatic use of the knowledge or information acquired requires rationality. Knowing how to dialogue and listen actively by summarizing, acknowledging and asking non-challenging questions facilitates safe spaces for learning about differences. Through emotional literacy, people exercise confidence and assertiveness to voice and take action. Being emotionally intelligent also enable people to recognize and manage feelings of distress and pain when listening to conflicting narratives or ideas. Knowing how to collaborate with others and when to reflect individually also empowers people in being citizens who effectively capitalize on the diversity of ideas and resources. Disabling people from accessing, learning or developing literacies merely oppresses them into fearful and, eventually, submissive citizens (Freire 1970).

Active citizens are *engaged* in the various communities they live in. At home or in the community, they are role models that inspire peers, elders or younger people. They collaborate with others when proactively organizing campaigns that raise awareness or provide social services for vulnerable people in need. Their efforts to support and learn extend to communities beyond their own, reaching those who not only have different beliefs and backgrounds but are perceived as perpetrators to social injustice or a history of violent conflict.

The active engagement of young people in communities transitioning out of conflict is critical to the building of new relationships and reconciliation of damaged ones. However, their status as children often marginalize and exclude them from opportunities to engage. Other times, they are assigned roles of engagement – like painting a mural of peace that teachers or politicians had designed – that undermine any conceptualization of an active citizen for living together. Across the surprisingly few conceptual frameworks on active participation or participation for active citizenship (Hart 1992; Kirby et al. 2003; Shier 2001; Treseder 1997), children who lead with peers or adults in planning and implementing activities experience levels of engagement that, in turn, empower them as agents of change. When a group of young teenagers in the Isle of Wight (UK) were given the opportunity to improve their community and share their progress using photographs and a web-based forum, they created their own recreational spaces despite feeling marginalized from the community in general (Weller 2007).

This intricate combination of principles, knowledge and participation leads to what Parker (2004) describes as 'enlightened political engagement' (33). Similarly, the three facets to active citizenship presented here that define degrees of agency must work in tandem. When trying to manage conflict, for example, active citizens learn about the conflict and their individual roles as a 'third side' who can intervene (Ury 2000). Being able to read the stage of conflict and decide what role they can most appropriately assume empowers them with the confidence and tools necessary to engage in an effective intervention between the conflicting parties. As another scenario, opportunities to engage are often limited to those who are in positional power like males and adults while vulnerable groups may be limited according to their status like young people under 18 (or 21), migrants and forcibly displaced people. This population can actively engage with community affairs when empowered through confidence and literacy. People with more privileged statuses can facilitate opportunities for vulnerable people to actively participate or engage in their communities by learning how to actively listen and dialogue about sensitive issues like transparency, lowering the voting age and human rights of refugees.

3

Effective Learning for Active Citizenship

In 2016, Nadine welcomed me to observe a number of lessons in her civic education classroom in a school in the South Lebanon governorate. For one of the lessons, the students moved their tables and debated whether child soldiers should be seen as victims or perpetrators. They had spent two weeks already preparing for this activity. Nadine created a safe space and designed dialogic pedagogies that engaged her students as citizens-in-action who discussed sensitive issues and learned more about others' positions that conflicted with their own (Akar 2017b). Unfortunately, this classroom was an exception. The empirical field is saturated with evidence of classroom practices that limit and even undermine the learning of active citizenship for democratic living and social cohesion.

This chapter closely examines the approaches to learning that can effectively foster an active notion of citizenship for living together. Any discourse that defines and examines the effectiveness of learning must conjoin pedagogical approaches with the desired outcomes to see if, how and how much the learning activities indeed help learners achieve the stated objectives. Therefore, developing a framework of effective learning for active citizenship begins with answering the question that Watkins, Carnell and Lodge (2007) present as foundational, 'Effective for what?' In the case of citizenship education, the 'what' is the set of indicators that define active citizenship. Chapter 2 presented some of these indicators, which include the ability to express conflict constructively, being informed of injustices in one's local and global communities, collaborating with people from different backgrounds and able to enquire when learning about differences. Hence, this chapter aims to outline a pedagogical framework of approaches that effectively inform, engage and empower young people as active citizens. For this framework, I present concepts of effective learning and active participation, draw on principles and practices of dialogic pedagogies, address the dominant practice of learning by rote and contextualize effective learning within traditions of learning in West Asia and North Africa shaped by religion and politics.

The various pedagogical orientations of this framework share the ontological position that young people learning to live as active young citizens require educational experiences based on a pragmatist philosophy of education. Pragmatists in education philosophy like John Dewey and William James argued that knowledge is a result of how learners address current issues together. Through pragmatism, learners begin with questions about themselves and their communities. They construct knowledge with peers that enable them to answer those questions and reflect on their learning experiences. In near-stark contrast, an essentialist philosophy of education views knowledge as almost absolute substance that authorities like governments and curriculum developers determine a priori. The same applies to character; essentialists believe in a defined set of character traits, which largely overlooks individual differences and even undermines a respect for diversity. Although learners through this world-dominant essentialist philosophy of education can make connections with topical issues, the selected bodies of content knowledge remain static over time until authorities produce a new set of information to learn. Education for active citizenship, therefore, requires a pragmatist ontology, which views learners as inquisitive and competent in co-constructing knowledge through critical pedagogies.

Effective learning and active participation

At the turn of the twenty-first century, pedagogues like Chris Watkins and his colleagues at the UCL Institute of Education brought together evidence from education and psychology research around the world to suggest four dimensions to effective learning: active learning, collaborative learning, learner-driven learning and meta-learning. These processes effectively empower learners to adapt to different and changing contexts, access and make sense of new information and work with people who bring in a diversity of ideas and approaches (Watkins, Carnell, and Lodge 2007). They not only define foundations of lifelong learning but also overlap with active conceptions of citizenship for living together. Indeed, core elements from these four approaches, such as working with others to create new understandings and learning about how we learn, are among the concepts that constitute the four pillars of education for learning to live together (Delors et al. 1996).

Active learning

Active learning happens when learners make sense of feedback on what they produced and reflections on how they produced it in order to improve the same or a different task. The term 'active' can mislead many to thinking that the learner is active by doing or participating in order to gain hands-on experience. However, through active learning, the learning is active; doing is only a part of the process. According to Dennison and Kirk's (1990) cyclical model of active learning, the doing happens first, followed by a process of review to formatively assess the outcome and process, then a period to learn or make sense of the feedback and then to apply what was learned either on the same or a different task. Watkins, Carnell, and Lodge (2007) added a planning stage prior to doing the activity. Time dedicated to planning allows learners to draw on previous knowledge and negotiate with others on how to go about the task. The overall process of Do-Review-Learn-Apply suggests that teachers allow learners to [co] construct the concepts or content knowledge rather than provide them with the information from the start. In practice, learning actively about the UNCRC as provisions, protection and participation could look like the following:

Plan: Each of the cards provided describes one UNCRC article. Read through them and start to think about which articles are similar to each other.
Do: In twos or threes, agree on which cards can be grouped together and what name you would give that category.
Review: Present the categories to the class. Invite comments from the teacher and peers.
Learn: Think about the feedback and presentation and reconsider how the cards were categorized.
Apply: Make any changes that further clarify, justify or explain how we can understand the articles of the UNCRC.

Active learning, therefore, emphasizes the *learning* as being active by gathering feedback and self-assessing the work and reflecting on their meanings for the next task. Experiencing this reflexive process fosters what Dewey (1938) describes as the 'democratic ideal' (33) and 'humane' methods (34) of schooling and knowledge building. The absence of feedback that encourages learners to review the task and think about ways to take the outcome to a higher level suggests an education that reinforces uncritical compliance. Active learning enhances the construction of content knowledge that informs learners about key concepts, instruments, events and issues. Trying a task for the first time with minimal pre-task input from the teacher empowers young people to express their views and engages them in practising their right to freely express their ideas, a pedagogical threat to authoritarian regimes. Moreover, the overall process of expecting and even seeking review – whether in the form of feedback or self-reflection – nurtures a degree of humility essential for respecting and even capitalizing on different perspectives.

Collaborative learning

Working and learning with peers opens opportunities to benefit from different ideas and experiences and, equally if not more important, develop the socio-emotional capacities to engage with others who may hold conflicting views and approaches. Through collaboration, learners co-construct knowledge, such as a solution to a problem or an explanation to a phenomenon. They work towards a common goal or task, one they may need to negotiate to agree on. In addition, each learner brings in a meaning or understanding of knowledge that peers dialogically explore in order to use for their shared task. Much discourse on core concepts of collaborative learning makes reference to cooperation. While some view collaboration and cooperation as synonymous (e.g. Gillies 2017), others have identified their conceptual differences (e.g. Tolmie et al. 2010). Despite the overlapping imagery of children working together, peers cooperate to help each other present a completed product like building the backdrop of a play or by sharing work they have individually completed. Collaboration yields a product shaped by the continuous input and negotiations among peers, one that would have looked very different from what each may have individually constructed.

Collaborative learning activities like reciprocal teaching (Palinscar and Brown 1984) and jigsaw (Aronson et al. 1978) gained popularity decades ago and teachers and researchers continue to advance their approaches in classrooms today. Secondary school students can use jigsaw to organize after-school learning support for migrant children forcibly displaced from war: one person would learn about the effects of trauma on child development, another on approaches to provide rehabilitative support, another on approaches to learning a second language and another on the cultural backgrounds of the children that have migrated. These four would come together to design approaches that could provide the necessary psychosocial and cognitive support needed to learn the language of the host community. The facilitation of small group work, however, must be carefully orchestrated. Learners can easily fall into disputes when learning together (Näykki et al. 2014). They may choose not to manage or address their conflicts and, as a result, commit less to their group members or the task. Some may loaf while overachievers could monopolize the tasks in fear of a low grade. Like learning any new and challenging methodology, learners require guidance on managing power relations among group members, regulating emotions, actively listening to peers, encouraging less engaging peers to participate and justifying ideas using evidence.

Co-constructing knowledge with peers creates learning experiences that enhance the learning of knowledge and support social, emotional and moral development. Learners who engage in exploratory conversations during collaborative problem-solving score higher on standardized tests assessing individual reasoning abilities (Wegerif, Mercer, and Dawes 1999). Collaborative learning activities that require critical dialogic interactions also generate communities of learners and enhance how young people learn disciplinary knowledge (Brown 1994). For active citizenship, collaboration provides a potentially ideal pedagogical setting that young people can learn through and from. Young people become empowered with the autonomy to develop moral knowledge and reasoning when collaborative activities safeguard learners from authoritative relations within the group (Leman and Duveen 1999). Collaborative learning experiences become even more critical when learning to live together in areas affected by armed conflict. In such contexts, young people bring to the classroom narratives and experiences that are very likely to conflict with or offend each other's values or commitments to religious sects and political parties. With careful guidance, structure and continuous reflections, young people can learn to recognize others' emotions, regulate their own, momentarily disengage their personal positions from the shared task and acknowledge ideas that conflict with their own.

Meta-learning

In defining 'Learning to know' as one of the four pillars of education (Delors et al. 1996), the authors underscored the importance of children developing 'the ability to learn how to learn' (19) in order to gain as much as they can from the educational opportunities provided through school and adult life. Meta-learning then gained front seat status in education policy frameworks when the European Parliament and Council (2006) approved the recommendation of learning to learn as one of eight key competencies for lifelong learning. Learning about how we learn, or meta-learning, is a critical yet often overlooked process that empowers the learner with the capacity to benefit from even the most challenging of learning contexts. Students who think and talk about their own learning are able to perform better and learn better because they use their understandings to make decisions that enhance their learning processes, experiences and performance (Watkins et al. 2001).

Having more control over how we learn addresses the harms associated with using learning styles to support student learning. Meta-analyses of decades of research on the use and influences of learning styles (Coffield et al. 2004a, b) suggest that teachers and learners can easily fall into the trap of tailoring learning activities per child's preference. While this surely facilitates learning for the students, it also handicaps them from developing approaches to benefiting from more challenging contexts. In reality, people are rarely provided with the resources and contexts they consider as ideal for learning and work. Hence, meta-learning empowers learners who, for example, prefer to work on their own to develop strategies that also yield a beneficial learning experience when working with others.

Learning to learn or, at least, about one's learning happens when we ask questions about the learning experience and how it can improve how we learn in later activities. According to Watkins (2015), learners can begin by asking what they notice about the activity and how they are doing it, then to narrate the learning experience – which generates a language of learning – and then to explain how they will continue to navigate through their journey of learning. As a result, young people take charge of experimenting with their learning like an action research project following the cyclical process of Dennison and Kirk's (1990) active learning. Moreover, teachers can engage children as young as 3 to 5 (pre-school) in conversations and reflections that support their learning about how they learn (Pramling 1990).

The processes and outcomes of meta-learning generate experiences that empower people as agents of change. Learners develop agency and responsibility when they critically reflect on their learning and regulate their learning environment. The learner with agency will also most likely think and behave as a citizen with agency. The helpless learner (i.e. I can work only with a partner who listens) resembles the submissive citizen (i.e. Why should I pay taxes when government officials avoid them?) while the autonomous and responsible learner (i.e. I reflect with my partners on how we listen to each other) mirrors the empowered and informed citizen (i.e. By declaring my taxes, I can confidently talk about good governance and corruption). Taking control of one's learning can encourage approaches that strengthen how we work and learn with other people, like being assertive while respectful and open-minded when discovering new things about peers. Learning to learn and active citizenship were found to represent 'two sides of the same coin' because young people using both competencies take decisions based on their reflections 'to control the direction' of their work, which enhances lifelong learning and sustainable living (Hoskins and Crick 2010, 130).

Learner-driven learning

Descriptions of classrooms have extended beyond teacher-centred or student-centred to focus more on learning (learning-centred) and the learner (learner-centred, learner-driven). The difference between '-centred' and '-driven' lies in agency, authority and responsibility. I illustrate this difference by referring to driving a car as a metaphor. Albeit the two place the learner in the front of the car (with seatbelts, of course), the former keeps the teacher in the driving seat while the latter places the learner behind the wheel next to the teacher. In the driving seat, learners have *a* say – rather than total control – in what they learn, how they learn it and what would best assess their learning and when (Watkins, Carnell, and Lodge 2007). For instance, learners would have a little more control of how much time they want to spend discussing with a partner or ask for some individual thinking time when working in a group and when they would like feedback on the work-in-progress and for which part of the work.

Encouraging learners to explain why the activity or topic might be important, discuss what they plan to do with the outcome, plan activities they have found to be most beneficial, asking questions they find most critical and think about where they can find answers or more information foster intrinsic motivators that enhance autonomy and academic achievement. Self-determination theory (Ryan and Deci 2000, Cerasoli, Nicklin, and Ford 2014) helps us understand how and why intrinsic motivation is so powerful to learning and learners (Vansteenkiste, Lens, and Deci 2006). Learners internally generate intrinsic motivation when teachers facilitate learning activities that meet their psychological needs of being challenged (competence), voicing purposes and directions of the learning activity (autonomy) and feeling listened to (relatedness) (Niemiec and Ryan 2009). When learners experience these opportunities, they are more actively engaged than those extrinsically motivated (Benware and Deci 1984) and can effectively apply their knowledge to new contexts in the absence of the teacher (Boggiano et al. 1993). In other words, learning activities that nurture young people's active voices about their learning are effective and sustainable through long-lasting commitments to improve and discover.

Encouraging learners to sit in the driving seat of their own learning mirrors the integrity and high levels of engagement and empowerment of active citizens fostering democratic living and social justice. A commitment to solve problems and focus on the quality of the outcome in the absence of teachers for instruction, grades and praise demonstrates integrity. People with high levels of integrity make decisions based on codes of ethics and a values system that upholds honesty and impartiality. Young people making decisions with teachers about their learning is an inclusive activity and narrows the social injustices of educational factors that marginalize vulnerable children. At-risk learners who discussed and agreed on learning activities with their teachers scored significantly higher on achievement tests than similar learners in a traditional remedial program (Niemiec and Ryan 2009). Furthermore, people are empowered when they are autonomous by making their own decisions and express high levels of confidence in their work (Thomas and Velthouse 1990); hence, young people can develop this capacity of empowerment that can help become better learners, collaborators, listeners and investigators. Learners' choices also result in richer questions and more relevant connections between concepts and reality. Through the learning activities, they engage more with ethical dilemmas and social injustices that teachers and curriculum makers exclude or avoid in schoolbooks that traditionally present content information and ideals. Moreover, their defined purposes can include advocacy work and connect more with the community, which expands their audience to beyond their teachers, parents and principal.

Active participation

The school is by design and default a community where young people develop their orientations of citizenship. These orientations are shaped by the degrees and forms of participation in the classroom, playground, library, gym, canteen and social and cultural activities organized through the school. A citizenship characterized by young people taking initiative, exploring different cultures, addressing human rights issues and working with each other regardless of age and ability is fostered when they *practise* living as active citizens in school. Dewey (1897) voiced this precise vision of education as 'a process of living and not a preparation of future living' (7). Thus, active participation through schooling in the form of *living* as active citizens is closely demonstrated within a pragmatist philosophy of education, but undermined by an essentialist one. Pragmatists like William James and John Dewey expect the methods and substance of knowledge construction to have a direct or purposeful relation with young people's realities (experiences, concerns, environment, etc.). The more conservative approaches of essentialism (e.g. Bagley 1905; Hirsch 1988) predetermine what content knowledge and elements of good character should be learned regardless of their real-time and socially constructed realities. Table 3.1 illustrates how these two philosophies manifest contrasting and even conflicting forms and degrees of participation.

Among the few frameworks that define degrees of active participation reflecting democratic and human rights principles, Roger Hart's (1992) metaphor of an eight-rung ladder has emerged as among the most influential. The bottom three steps describe forms of participation that undermine democratic engagement and notions of agency and, thus, are defined as 'non-participation'. Under manipulation, for example, children receive no information on why they are doing something and how their ideas are being used (i.e. teachers ask children to draw a dream playground that may be later considered but without the children's knowledge). As decoration, the initiative is explicitly from adults, but children

Table 3.1 Participation of young people (YP) within pragmatist and essentialist frameworks

Activities	Pragmatism	Essentialism
Conducting a science experiment	YP notice phenomenon, design experiment together and interpret results; teacher gives feedback.	YP follow planned experiment in science book and compare results with book; teacher gives instructions.
Examining a violation of human rights in the news	YP extract human rights issues from media, observations or experiences; YP look at HRI beyond national borders.	Book presents text on human rights issue (HRI) for YP to read; HRI is mostly injustice to national citizens and country.
Organizing a food and clothes drive	YP identify most needy, advertise collection point and date and, with support from teacher, coordinate with NGO.	School selects and arranges activity with NGO. YP are asked to bring food and clothes to school.
Preparing a cultural performance	YP and teacher agree on and choreograph performance; YP celebrate diversity of cultures from around the world.	YP perform dance or play selected and choreographed by teachers; YP celebrate elements of national identity.

participate for emotional appeal (i.e. performing a dance or song selected and choreographed by an adult). Thirdly, participation becomes tokenistic when children communicate with others but the subject was not their idea, nor was the way of communicating it (i.e. carrying out an awareness-raising campaign designed completely by adults to fulfil community service hours).

The five higher rungs of the ladder define expressions of active participation varying in degrees of how much (1) adults inform and consult children and (2) children initiate and share decisions with adults. Hart (2008), however, cautions against misinterpreting features of the ladder. The rungs should not suggest levels of participation that children begin with at the bottom and climb to the top. Moreover, the higher steps are merely different degrees, all of which respect the child's right to engage according to their will. He explains the highest rung where children have the most decision-making powers and initiative as the least observed. Subsequent frameworks (e.g. Shier 2001; Treseder 1997) have also illustrated degrees of participation from less desirable to more desirable when striving for an active form of citizenship. Kirby et al. (2003), however, focused more on observing the nature and frequency of participation when (1) taking children's views into account, (2) involving children in decision-making, (3) children sharing power and responsibility and (4) children making autonomous decisions.

The schooling experience for active citizenship becomes extremely powerful when active participation and approaches to effective learning are integrated in classroom and extra-curricular learning activities like student councils, intercultural collaborations and community service. This continuity creates the school as a community that holistically facilitates the cognitive and socio-emotional areas of human growth and development for active citizenship. Children in such a school live as active citizens who not only actualize their human rights but also develop the relationships, language and approaches to living with others who bring different and even conflicting perspectives.

Dialogue as pedagogy for learning to live together

On 14 July 2015, the world witnessed the power of dialogue as a diplomatic tool that negotiated a deal between Iran and the International Atomic Energy Agency over Iran's nuclear program. Over a period of 2 years, Iranian government officials met with representatives of the five permanent UN Security Council members (China, France, UK, United States and Russia) and Germany to agree on mechanisms that ensure the nature of Iran's nuclear activities are peaceful in return for the relief of sanctions that have hampered Iran's economic growth. Even the formation of this platform and gathering of representatives from the United States and Iran proved extremely controversial among their allies and partisans who protested against these meetings. Learning about such settlements and treaties negotiated through talk – whether at an international or local scale – illustrate the significance and applications of dialogues in transforming potentially destructive expressions of conflict into constructive ones.

Young people engaging and learning to engage in powerful dialogues are instrumental for at least three competencies necessary to live as active citizens within diverse communities. First, dialogues allow people to acknowledge differences and even capitalize on them. When individuals work together in a group, they bring in different experiences and approaches that are likely to clash with each other but, through support, result in outputs rich in ideas they could not have built individually. Conflicting values, experiences and perspectives are also inevitable in public or private discourse on daily issues like the news, a different group of people who just moved in to the neighbourhood, the cost of mobile phone contracts and how the local municipality is managing waste. Through dialogues, people engage in emotionally and cognitively challenging tasks of asking each other questions of enquiry, rephrasing each other's positions and finding sound evidence to support their own claims. These conversations, however, generate new understandings, consensus or even an agreed recognition of differences.

Secondly, people practise their freedoms when they voice their positions or invite others to do the same. Exercising the human right to form and express opinions and enquire about others (UDHR, article 10; UNCRC, article 13) is a collective action for liberation, social justice and critical thinking and, thus, particularly significant for vulnerable groups like children and others from marginalized communities (Freire 1970; Giroux 2001).

Thirdly, dialogues enrich learning activities that foster lifelong learning. Some competencies of lifelong learning include teamwork, creativity, problem-solving and being empowered to contribute to safe, just and inclusive communities (European Commission 2018). Through dialogues in the classroom, learners think collectively (Mercer 2000), construct knowledge together when talking during social activities (Mercer 1995) and engage in 'reflection, critical investigation, analysis, interpretation and reorganization of knowledge' and 'complex understandings' (Carnell and Lodge 2002, 15).

Watkins (2005) emphasizes a powerful effect of dialogue in learning where 'authentic interchange ... generates new understandings and possibilities' (121).

Learning to engage in dialogues is, therefore, a foundational cross-curricular dimension to any educational programme designed to empower and engage children as active citizens. Citizenship education in democratic societies is one of many opportunities because of its nature to address topical issues. Facilitating these difficult conversations inside a classroom may indeed be the only opportunity for young people to receive guidance in generating constructive expressions of conflict, acting on their freedoms and fostering lifelong learning, especially in areas affected by conflict. In order to design dialogic pedagogies that effectively lead to better understandings of other peoples' different positions or even consensus, teachers must view knowledge as a product of young people's co-constructions rather than absolute (Akar 2016) and collaborate as co-learners with young people in the classroom by exchanging questions and encouraging curiosity (Freire and Faundez 1989).

The antithesis of dialogic pedagogy is an education of answers deemed as 'correct', narratives presented as official and a world in an ideal form. When teachers ask questions like, 'Who do you call when you have a problem in your community?' expecting a correct answer like, 'the police', they subject children to rhetorical dialogues. Rhetorical dialogues foster conformity, prevent opportunities for critically reflecting on topical issues and, in extreme cases, even stigmatize critical discourse. Questions that seek correct answers tell children that we should strive to create a perfect world without addressing environments that undermine dignified living. Moreover, classrooms that avoid these issues exercise censorship and authoritarianism by dictating what we should and should not discuss. This closely resembles an essentialist approach to education that delivers a close-ended curriculum of static knowledge for learners to recite when assessed. In stark contrast, a pragmatist philosophy of education views dialogue as a means to manage the diversities of ideas and values. What dialogues for learning to live together also do not do is convince others of a view or win arguments. Although debate is a form of dialogic activity, the aim of debates to demonstrate an idea is more convincing than another contradicts the pragmatics of dialogue for understanding why others may hold different or even conflicting views.

Dialogic activities can be 'dangerous' because people engaging in genuine dialogues 'reveal ... their deepest interests, hopes and fears', which make them vulnerable (Saunders 1999, 84). Inside the classroom, debates and discussions will most likely create tensions and even trigger conflicts that can agitate and trouble students (DeCuir-Gunby and Williams 2007) and teachers (Zembylas et al. 2011). Managing emotions in the classroom is, therefore, integral to engaging in dialogic activities.

Emotionality and learning

Literature on approaches to learning, teaching and active participation often overlooks the affective dimension that enriches and challenges learning experiences. Learners and teachers come to class already with emotions charged from home or the teachers' room. Young people sometimes experience feelings of infatuation towards a peer that can either motivate or distract them from learning activities. Conflicts with a parent or sibling at home can damage the drive to participate in class. Emotions are also influenced by routine school-related events, including fear from encountering a bully, chronic stress from systematic summative assessment and feeling rejected from teachers or peers. Teachers are often unmindful of how emotionally vulnerable learners are to their teachers' approval, acceptance and affection; indeed, many become consumed with finding the right answer (and finding it fast) and, when they do not, are easily subject to feelings of guilt, failure and rejection (Moore 2013). In addition to these, learning activities that touch on issues perceived as sensitive or controversial will trigger feelings associated with injustice, pride, experiences and collective memories. It is within this sensitive and complex pedagogic context that I underscore emotionality as a critical dimension to learning citizenship.

The affective dimension in citizenship education can either foster or undermine active citizenship. When living as active citizens in formal and non-formal educational settings, learners reflect on social injustices and listen to conflicting narratives or viewpoints. In areas affected by armed conflict, the classroom is diverse with learners who have either experienced first-hand forced displacement and direct violence, inherited a collective memory of suffering and struggle or even a generation with virtually no exposure to war-related loss or trauma. Hence, almost any learner in a conflict-affected area is vulnerable to feelings of stress, discomfort, anxiety, shock, anger, betrayal and helplessness when reading narratives and watching video testimonies of victims and perpetrators and exchanging ideas and experiences through dialogues on social injustice and reconciliation. Conversations and learning activities in the classroom could quite easily uncover opposing accounts of a violent past and personal experiences of loss, direct violence and marginalization. Teachers in such contexts fear facilitating discussions over controversial or sensitive issues in case they trigger feelings that could fuel destructive expressions of conflict; thus, teachers prefer to avoid them altogether and focus more on the transmission of knowledge prepared by a higher authority (Quaynor 2012; Weinstein, Freedman, and Hughson 2007). While trying to prevent potential conflicts erupting from dialogues, teachers with narrowed constructs of a highly nationalistic citizenship instead appeal to emotional narratives and stirring symbols to promote a non-negotiable sense of loyalty or patriotism. An education that creates an emotion-based attachment to a nation undermines a citizenship formed through critical and rational thought, excludes voices of minority groups and 'reduces the space for democratic debate' (Starkey 2018, 10).

Ironically, pedagogies for active citizenship that intend to do no harm, indeed, risk depriving young people from possibly the only space that can address controversial and sensitive issues while supporting them to understand others' feelings, manage their own, listen actively and construct arguments based on sound evidence. A citizenship education that does provide this safe and inclusive space will inform and empower young people to carefully manage difficult explorations and encounters and direct them towards constructive expressions like empathy, consensus and even acknowledging differences.

Designing and facilitating learning activities that critically examine sensitive and controversial issues are emotionally demanding and daunting experiences for teachers (Hayward 2009; Zembylas et al. 2011). It is quite difficult for teachers to separate their personal experiences and values from how they select the topics and sources to explore in the classroom, how impartial they remain throughout the activities and support the learners' and their own emotions triggered from the conversations or sources. Being sensitive to conflicts generated through learning activities, whether inside or outside the classroom, requires a great degree of awareness and preparation to support learners recognizing these emotions and trying ways to manage them. Without the appropriate support for listening actively (e.g. asking questions, summarizing, acknowledging another's position), identifying and expressing one's feelings and exercising empathy, encounters with different and conflicting views become vulnerable to destructive expressions of conflict.

Traditions of pedagogy in West Asia and North Africa

The concepts that enrich and even define approaches of learning to live together – collaboration, reflection, autonomy, feedback, dialogue, active participation – have been mostly drawn from traditions of education developed by educationists in Western Europe and North and South America. In this exploration on citizenship education in areas affected by conflict, however, the case of Lebanon lies in a region of the world that has a distinctive culture and history. Even the regard towards dialogue cannot be taken for granted. Scholars in the Arab region have described dialogue as a Western [*sic*] invention used to stall attempts at resolving conflict. Siddiqui (1997) supports this notion with the view that the Holy Qur'ān remains the absolute scripture, thus creating a level of mistrust towards Western [*sic*] dialogues. However, Islamic scholars like Al-Jirari (2000) have claimed Islam to be 'the religion of dialogue' (9). Khātami (2000), a former President of Iran, stressed on the importance of dialogue for rational and critical thinking in intellectual and even religious matters.

In West Asia and North Africa, practices of teaching and learning in modern-day classrooms have been largely shaped by early Islamic traditions of knowledge-building, political movements of the Ottoman Empire and post-colonial national reform. The first period took place between the late seventh and thirteenth centuries. Some refer to this period as the Arab Enlightenment (Massialas and Jarrar 1983), the Classical Period (Khalidi 1985) or the Golden Age of Islam (Al-Djazairi 2006; Lombard 1975). This age of scholarship and trade led to the rise of universities, libraries and research institutions in Baghdad, Cairo, Damascus, Palestine, Cordoba and Sicily (Al-Djazairi 2006). Moreover, the pedagogies of religious education at the start of the era grounded the foundations of learning (Massialas and Jarrar 1983) from which 'early Muslim scholars' had 'originated many psychological theories and practices prevalent today' (Haque 2004, 360). However, Mongol invasions in the thirteenth century destroyed knowledge hubs like Baghdad, libraries and science institutions. Soon after in the fourteenth century, the Ottoman Empire rose and took power. Its administrative regimes enforced a more authoritarian approach to learning, teaching and school governance. The second period took place towards the end of the Ottoman Empire and through the early twentieth-century post-colonial movements of nations and nation-states. The political agendas of these movements strengthened the emphasis of reciting information officiated by government authorities. The events during these two periods show how the uncritical transference of knowledge is deeply embedded into the religious and political cultures in West Asia and North Africa, despite traditions of collaboration, reflection and dialogue.

Early Islamic culture and pedagogy

Islamic doctrine has regarded the attainment of knowledge as fundamental means to bring humans closer to understanding God and community cohesion and growth. In *hadīth*, the collected writings on the Prophet's life, Prophet Muhammad [Peace be upon him] was said to 'seek knowledge from the cradle to the grave' and 'search for knowledge as far as China'. The Prophet not only spoke of ignorance as sin, but also declared the search for knowledge as a religious duty for all Muslims, men and women (Mohammed 2005). Narrow and distorted interpretations of Islam, however, have dismissed knowledge from non-Islamic culture as blasphemous and even forbid females from accessing education. These interpretations counter Islam's fundamental values of inclusion (Tibi 2004) and the lifelong commitment to learning through continuous gathering of evidence, logical reasoning and reflection (Kamis and Muhammad 2007). From within the embracement of lifelong learning in Islam, foundational pedagogies of memorization, knowledge circles, modelling and reflection emerged.

Rote recitations of religious prayers and scripts were an important part of Torah reading in Judaism, reciting the Bible in Christianity and the Holy Qur'ān. Educators in the early years of Islam, however, sought other ways of learning. 'Realizing the shortcomings of repetition and memorization', a new approach emerged 'based on discussion and interaction among the learners and their peers and teachers' which would make learning 'more meaningful and would raise the level of understanding' (Massialas and Jarrar 1983, 13). This prompted the formation of discussion groups known as circles or *halaqāt*. Discussion groups also led to a culture of dialogue forming a *munāzarah*, or as Sadiki (2004) describes it, a forum of intellectuals during the Muslim enlightenment that practised the value of knowledge-seeking across other cultures.

Modelling the life of the Prophet also transpired into a main form of teaching and learning. In early Islamic education, the lifestyle, practices and sayings of the Prophet served as model behaviours. These practices or the path of the Prophet, known as *Sunna*, were recorded in text form known as *hadīth*. Through the *hadīth*, 'Muslims learn how to live their life by imitating how the prophet reportedly conducted his life' such as religious rituals like the pilgrimage to Mecca (Kamis and Muhammad 2007, 32). Reflection also became a valued practice of learning. Indeed, numerous verses in the Qur'ān ask individuals to 'travel the world so they can better reflect on their actions' (Kamis and Muhammad 2007).[1] Reflection and interpretation promote critical thinking, which become contested pedagogical practices for conservative views of reason challenging the divine attribute of religious scripture.

The relationships between approaches to learning and living in a diverse community were probably first explicitly reflected on by Ibn Khaldūn, a sociologist and historian in the fourteenth century. Ibn Khaldūn rejected memorization and, instead, argued for active practices of learning for the purposes of attaining the highest degree of intellect and for the development of skills necessary for practice and participation. Through observations, experiences and reflection, humans learn the skills and attitudes necessary for participation and solidarity. The three degrees of intellect begin with discerning, then experimental and then speculative (Ibn Khaldūn 2005 [1370]). In the first degree, humans obtain what is useful and reject what is harmful based on perceptions. In the second, humans develop behaviours necessary for interaction learned through experience. Ibn Khaldūn found that from our perceptions, we learn to seek or reject necessities for survival and through experiences we develop the behaviours required for interaction such as mutual affection, support, aid and cooperation. In the highest degree, speculative intellect combines perceptions and experiences for knowledge beyond activity and observations such as philosophy and existentialism. As part of the cognitive practices in processing these observations and experiences, Ibn Khaldūn rejected learning through memorization. Instead, he emphasized learning through habituation as a process 'different from understanding and knowing by memory' (Ibn Khaldūn 2005 [1370], 340). In addition, the mastery of skills through scientific habit requires rigour in debates and dialogues over scientific problems. The emphasis of habituation on participation and moral development suggests Aristotle's influence on Ibn Khaldūn, whom he referenced as the First Teacher.

Educators during the Golden Age used memorization, discussion circles and practices of the Prophet's life when teaching young people. These pedagogies further developed understandings of learning that suggested notions of short-term learning through memorization and more applicable outcomes from habituation and discussions. However, the rise of the Ottoman Empire in the

---

[1] Kamis and Muhammad (2007) make reference to verses 3:137 and 6:11. For more, see verses 2:266, 16:44, 16:69, 34:46 and 38:29.

1500s strengthened an even more centralized, authoritarian approach to teaching and learning inside the classroom that continues up until modern times.

National governance through classroom pedagogy

Following the decline of the Arab Enlightenment, practices of learning and teaching were reshaped by political movements governing the region's territories. During the Ottoman Empire from the sixteenth to nineteenth centuries, education fell under administrative rule by religious institutions of the empire. By imposing an elementary education that focused mainly on reciting the Holy Qur'ān, writing and arithmetic, the Ottoman Empire isolated the Arab Islamic civilization from the Renaissance, Reformation and Industrial Revolution (Massialas and Jarrar 1983). Furthermore, the Ottoman Empire's highly bureaucratic administrative systems reinforced orthodox approaches to learning information in order to pass its official exams. Hence, as Massialas and Jarrar (1983) found, 'memory work' was accepted as the main mode of instruction in order to accurately recall information for the final exams (109). The pedagogical establishment of rote learning was sustained throughout the fall of the Ottoman Empire and further reinforced during the colonial mandates after the First World War.

The French mandate ensured its domination over Greater Lebanon by creating an education system that would ensure the subjugation of the people of Greater Lebanon. The mandate enforced French as an official language of instruction alongside Arabic, prevented the establishment of public secondary schools in Beirut and created an official exam that virtually no student had passed (Sbaiti 2015). For over two decades of French rule, the pedagogical traditions to instil loyalty and other emotional ties towards France were threatened by any educational activities that critically discussed the social and political life under colonial governance. A similar drive of nationalism was then pursued through the government of Lebanon as a republic after the mandate. The battle for Lebanese nationalism was apparent in the first national curriculum that reinstated Arabic as the official language with French and English as secondary and produced civics, history and geography curricula that celebrated Lebanese heritage, rights and identity (Frayha 1985). However, Massialas and Jarrar (1983) explained that the Lebanese nationalist reforms to demonstrate autonomy and sovereignty resulted in replacing foreign teachers with any individual willing to teach as long as they had national legal status. This move even further institutionalized rote learning because teachers would design their lessons as drills to recite content from previous exams and, hence, claimed authority of the subject they taught (Massialas and Jarrar 1983).

Practices of learning through discussions, collaboration, construction and reflection were among the methods of knowledge production in the region surrounding Lebanon over a millennium ago. The rise and fall of colonial political movements and the competition for winning allegiance placed the formation of national citizenship as a fundamental aim of education. The governing administrations believed that constructing an uncritical and submissive citizenry could most effectively be achieved through the drilling of narratives that celebrated national heritage in its language and cultural symbols. 'The mere memorization of information [that] has been, and still is, the strategy underlying the methodology of the pedagogical system in Arab-Muslim countries' (Hankiss 2004, 201) also appears in classrooms of other conflict-affected areas around the world. Studies on learning and teaching citizenship in Rwanda, Bosnia and Herzegovina, Croatia, provinces in Kosovo (Weinstein, Freedman, and Hughson 2007), Tunisia and Egypt (Faour and Muasher 2011) show that teachers dictate single narratives and ideals for children to recite later despite the values for critical thinking, collaboration and dialogic activities expressed in education policy rhetoric. Throughout the rest of this book, I further explore how teachers and young learners in school manage engaging in critical pedagogies and, consequently, the position of formal citizenship education in fostering young citizens who are informed, engaged and empowered.

Part Two

Citizenship Education in Lebanon in Rhetoric and Reality

Lebanon: Education Policy in Times of Conflict and Change

A metaphor for diversity

History and political and social science research on Lebanon commonly make reference to the metaphor of a mosaic to describe the country's state of religious diversity. The descriptions convey a sense of admiration in how the Government of Lebanon recognizes eighteen religious communities of Lebanese citizens (Alawite, Armenian Catholic, Armenian Orthodox, Assyrian Church of the East, Chaldean Catholic, Copt, Druze, Greek Catholic, Greek Orthodox, Isma'ili, Jewish, Maronite Catholic, Protestant, Roman Catholic, Sunni, Shi'a, Syriac Catholic, Syriac Orthodox) and how they live together in a nation-state of only 10,452 square kilometres. The cultural diversity of Lebanon evolved over five millennia of trade and education. In 3000 BC, Lebanon was occupied by a mix of people from the Arabian Desert and the Indo-European 'Sea Peoples' known as Canaanites whom the Greeks recognized as Phoenicians. During the Roman Empire, the Phoenician city-state was a centre of trade, worship, arts and education for people from parts of Asia, Europe and Africa. According to Hitti (1967), the Phoenicians traded with the Pharaohs of Egypt and taught the Greeks navigation, literature, religion and decorative art; Heliopolis's (known as Ba'albak) temple had achieved 'world-wide fame' where people worshipped the god of lighting and thunder and later the sun (214), and Roman Berytus (known as Beirut) established 'the most renowned provincial school of Roman law' which became a 'mecca for the legal minds of the entire East' (226–227).

In the seventh century, Islam was founded in Arabia and spread across the region. The Islamic faith and Arab ways of life transformed into the predominant culture. During the spread of Islam, Christian sects maintained their cultural practices and identities, but did so as minorities or second-class citizens. At the time, they could neither hold public office, nor wear turbans, nor have saddles on their horses and were not allowed to build places of worship (Hitti 1967). Meanwhile, a new religious sect – the Druze – had risen as a branch of Islam and spread throughout the eleventh and twelfth centuries. By the start of the Ottoman Empire in 1516, Lebanon had hosted an array of religious communities and cultures.

Cultural identities among Lebanese people extended beyond Lebanese and Arab nationalisms and their religious and political communities as they migrated to most parts of the world. The Lebanese diaspora is estimated between 6 and 8 million yet calculated at 4.5 million (Hourani, Haddad, and Sfeir 2011), almost the same population as Lebanese citizens inside Lebanon today. Although settled outside Lebanon, they participate in national political and economic activities including money transfers to support families and political parties, with remittances averaging a third of the nation's GDP (Tabar 2009). And, with a large population of Lebanese moving in and out of Lebanon, a vast number of Lebanese citizens carry hyphenated citizenship status of nations from around the world.

The image of a mosaic where carefully arranged distinctive tiles create a larger work of art gives recognition to each religious sect as a special, individual entity alongside others forming Lebanese and Arab identity schemes. This illustration eludes the notion of a melting pot, a metaphor commonly used to describe the assimilation of different cultures into one dominant group. The melting pot discourse in the United States, for example, intended to override ethnocultural diversity (Banks 1997), but it was also countered with the 'mixed salad' to argue that minority groups sharing the same community with a dominant national group can live together without having to compromise distinctive cultural identities and practices.

The discourse on conflict and social reconstruction in modern Lebanon, however, distorts the liberal and cosmopolitan principles outlined in the metaphor of a mosaic that celebrates pluralism and diversity. During the 1975–1990 civil war, warring religious and political communities published their own history education books that narrated conflicting accounts of heroes and perpetrators of violence (Salibi 1988). Also, students and teachers had brought degrees of anarchy to schools by joining militias for protection; as militia fighters and partisans, they showcased their allegiance to their parties through debates and graffiti, forged official school documentation and carried arms to school (BouJaoude and Ghaith 2006). These are only a few examples of how the 15-year civil war [further] stigmatized the diversity of ideas, narratives and identities. Hence, the 1990 Ta'if Accord – the 1975–1990 civil war peace treaty – called for unifying all history textbooks into one grand narrative. Almost two decades into the twenty-first century, school and university leaders in most educational institutions vehemently prohibit the self-expressions of religious and political identities in the classroom. These actions have institutionalized a cultural discourse that declares taboo the open expression of religious and political identities. What is more concerning, however, is the hasty attribution of diversity as a root to conflict and the subsequent call for nationalist ideologies to foster patriotism towards a predominant, unifying identity. In this chapter, I present various forms of conflict in Lebanon and their destructive expressions in Lebanon. I then outline how education policy reform attempted to address and transform the roots to conflict.

Armed and non-armed conflicts

Since its independence as a Republic in 1943, Lebanon has become ridden with a history and ongoing cultures and episodes of armed and non-armed forms of conflict. Wars, corruption, gender-based violence, unsustainable waste management and hostilities towards forcibly displaced people undermine the Government's commitment to universal instruments like the UHDR, UNCRC and CEDAW. These conflicts inspire movements that reform education for a citizenship of living together, but paradoxically threaten much of the impetus for educational change.

A site of armed conflicts

Religious and political armed conflicts in the past four decades have turned Lebanon into a high-tension conflict zone. Zakharia (2011) outlines a brief modern history of its armed struggles to illustrate the propensity for violence and other forms of aftermath conflicts such as unresolved grievances and deep-rooted sectarian tensions:

- The war of 1958: Resulted from attempts to increase government representation of Muslims in a confessional-based government system
- The 1975–1989 civil war: Battles among Lebanese religious and political militias, Palestinians, and armies from Israel and Syria left an estimated 200,000 dead and 17,000 missing persons
- The Qāna Massacre in 1996

- Israeli withdrawal from the South in 2000 leaving 430,000 unidentified ordnances (i.e. landmines)
- String of political assassinations in 2004–2008 killing ten politicians and scores of civilians
- July war of 2006: The 34-day Israeli offensive in Lebanon left 750,000 displaced persons and devastation to the environment including coastlines and farmland
- Sit-ins and protests in 2006–2007: Protests paralysing the government and the economy lasted 18 months and ended in riots in Beirut, Akkar and the Bekka
- Nahr-el Bared crisis in 2007: Violent armed clashes between the Lebanese Army and a militia group in a Palestinian refugee camp in Tripoli leaving displaced 26,000 Palestinians and 1,000 local residents
- Sectarian clashes in 2008 and 2011: In 2008, Hezbollah protested through shootings in West Beirut to government attempts to dismantle its communications network. In 2011, the civil war in Syria had spilled over into Tripoli with armed clashes between Muslim communities – Sunnis and Alawis.

As the war in Syria escalated, al-Nusra Front (a faction and later ally of the so-called Islamic State) gained control of Arsal, a village in northwest Lebanon bordering Syria. In 2014, al-Nusra Front took hostage sixteen Lebanese army and police officers who were later released. In August 2017, Hezbollah led an offensive with support from the Lebanese army and liberated the village. Albeit nearly three decades since the end of the 15-year civil war, the current state of war with Israel and the neighbouring wars maintain Lebanon's vulnerability to outbursts of armed violence, collective memories of injustice and a climate of insecurity and instability.

Lebanon is also situated in a region of ongoing wars and uprisings. The horrendous wars in Syria and Iraq in the twenty-first century and the ongoing occupation and apartheid in Palestine for over 70 years have situated Lebanon as a host to nearly two million people from Syria, Iraq and Palestine forcibly displaced by war and violence. According to the UNHCR (2016), Lebanon is among six countries that provide refuge to most of the forcibly displaced people in the world and hosts the largest number of refugees in the world per capita. The population of refugees in Lebanon comprises over 1.5 million people from Syria (Lebanon Crisis Response Plan 2015), some 450,000 from Palestine with over half living in the twelve camps across the country (UNRWA 2017) and around

50,000 from Iraq over the last decade, mostly Iraqi Christians (Caritas Lebanon Migrant Center 2014). While the Government of Lebanon has opened its borders for a population nearly half the number of Lebanese in the country, the influx and temporary settlement of refugees take place with great resistance and continuity of violence towards the forcibly displaced. Here, I outline only four levels of threat towards refugees. At one level, the dominant Lebanese nationalist discourse views the settlement of refugees as a threat to limited resources, including jobs, living spaces, electricity and water. Forcibly displaced Syrians are also a threat to the expatriated community of Syrian people who have settled in Lebanon prior to 2011 but still living in a degree of poverty as both communities compete for resources provided by civil society and international agencies. At the political level, the settlement of refugees (who constitute a majority of Muslims) threaten the Christian minority groups. Permanent settlement could involve naturalization and, thus, result in power shifts within the consociational model of democratic government. At the international policy and governance level, the Government of Lebanon has not ratified the 1951 Refugee Convention. Besides the resistance to permanently settling refugees, rejecting this convention is a form of protest to Israeli aggression and other State Parties of the convention who have exercised measures that counter their commitments towards refugees entering their territories (Janmyr 2017).

Political cultures of corruption and gender-based violence

Despite the explicit commitment to democracy and human rights in the Lebanese Constitution, the Republic is still ridden with a culture of corruption and social injustice. Lebanon's democracy is built on confessional and consociational principles. As a confessional democracy, government representation is based on a power-sharing formula across the religious and political communities (Mattar 2007, 49) who open declare their political and social agendas (Abouchedid 2008). Government representation is also formulated according to proportional distribution of sectarian identity and population. This system of consociational democracy fosters and strengthens political confessionalism and commonly appears in multi-ethnic societies (Nixon et al. 2007). However, the practices of confessional-consociational democracy in Lebanon has, in many cases, undermined democratic principles through nepotism and resistance to revise the power-sharing formula based on population demographics of religious sects. For example, the last official national census, which determined the current distribution of government representation, took place in 1932. Political reform following the 1990 Ta'if Accord recognized the controversies of political confessionalism and, thus, amended the Lebanese constitution through article 95 calling for the 'abolishment of political confessionalism', which 'shall be replaced by the principles of *expertise* and *competence*' (Lebanese Constitution 1997, 259–260, emphasis added by self). Article 95, however, makes exception to 'Grade One posts and their equivalents' to be still shared equally among Muslims and Christians but based on the same principles of expertise and competence.

The culture of corruption in Lebanon prevails, undercutting democratic living in Lebanon. According to the Corruption Perception Index 2017 reviewing 180 countries, Lebanon ranked 143 and scored 28 of 100, placing it more corrupt than nearby countries like Algeria (33), Egypt (32) and Iran (30) and countries of domestic workers in Lebanon including Ethiopia (35), Bangladesh (28) and Sri Lanka (38) (Transparency International 2018). Bribery in Lebanon allows for bureaucrats to speed up processing paperwork, erase outstanding utility bills or overlook building code violations. People in positional power and wealth have amended laws to expand construction sites, blocked opportunities for growing markets to compete against their goods and services, facilitate amnesty to drug and warlords and influenced senior administrators in education institutions to expedite their children's completion of secondary or higher education. Ironically, traditions of corruption institutionalized during the civil war damaged reconstruction processes and activities through the destruction of heritage sites that survived the war and the embezzlement of donor and government funds (Adwan 2004). Nepotism, or *wasta*, allows for people to benefit solely from connections, which resemble pre-Islamic tribal organizations. Wasta is contested as a form of corruption because not making exceptions to family or community members (providing jobs, supporting applications, ensuring release if arrested) can undermine the legitimacy of alliances and loyalty. Even young children conceptualize these connections as a critical component of citizenship as they bear witness to people in power employing relatives and helping them when in trouble (Joseph 2005).

Corruption has even damaged conditions for environmental sustainability. In Lebanon, mountains are mined by illegal quarries, waste is dumped into natural water resources and buildings are quickly constructed in urban green spaces. During the summer of 2015, the main landfill in Beirut was forced to close after exceeding its capacity considerably and mounds of garbage lined the streets. Triggering a nationwide garbage management crisis, a grassroots movement called 'You Stink' was formed and protested against corruption as a root to the unsustainable approaches to waste management. Environmental sustainability is also under threat by air pollution, waste dumping into the sea and controversial quarry sites. The UNDAF Report found that environmental issues continue to fall low on education and policy agendas (UNCT 2009), two arenas essential for addressing the intersection of corruption and sustainable living.

Lebanon stands as virtually the most liberal and democratic member state of the Arab League. We continue to find, however, that the structural and cultural violence towards women are similar to the other member states that retain women as second-class citizens through the laws and socially constructed gender roles that dictate divorce, inheritance, mobility and protection. Lebanese women married to non-Lebanese men cannot pass on their Lebanese citizenship status to their children. The prevention of naturalizing males who marry a national female is common in West Asia and North Africa (Meer and Sever 2004). Arguably, Christian political leaders heavily control the naturalization of Muslims because of the perceived potential threat of Muslims dominating nearly all government representative positions. Consequently, however, the denial of citizenship status to children from their mothers' results in a string of children's human rights violations, including the children's right to preserve their parent's national identity (UNCRC, Article 8) and State Party's provisions of quality education and healthcare (UNCRC, Article 24). The gendering of citizenship in West Asia and North Africa, and specifically Lebanon, not only dictates rights that benefit males, but also constructs *and* is constructed by the male-dominated political sphere. Lebanon is among the eight countries that have the least ratio of women representatives in national parliament in the world; ironically, more conservative countries in the region have a higher percentage of women in national parliament, like Iran (6 per cent), Syria (13 per cent), Egypt (15 per cent), Saudi Arabia (20 per cent) and Iraq (25 per cent) compared to Lebanon (3 per cent) (Inter-Parliamentary Union 2018). Moreover, nearly all women *in* political power in Lebanon achieved their positions through some connection from a male kin in power (Joseph 1999a), a structure that Joseph (1999b) describes as patriarchical lineality.

Corruption, gender-based violence and short-sighted management of the natural environment indicate a culture of unsustainable living. These are only some examples of latent and destructive expressions of conflict. This section could continue to illustrate other locations of conflict in Lebanon such as poverty, child soldiers, asbestos, destroying sites of ancient civilizations for new buildings, rare provisions of mobility for disabled people, criminalization of homosexuality and the additional tariffs on electric vehicles. What is possibly more concerning is the degree to which people in Lebanon have normalized or become habituated to these threats to sustainable living. Although they have neither significantly motivated nor triggered national policy reforms, the active political landscape has nevertheless produced a legal framework with universalistic principles and education reforms for social cohesion.

National policy and education reforms

Lebanon has stood at the forefront of embracing universal codes that strive for social justice, human dignity and environmental sustainability. In the Preamble of the Lebanese Constitution, the Government of Lebanon declared its commitment to the UDHR 'without exception' (Republic of Lebanon 1990) and ratified the UNCRC (children's human rights) and CEDAW (women's human rights), two legally binding instruments. Charles Malik, a Lebanese philosopher, politician and diplomat, co-led the writing of the UN's 1948 Universal Declaration of Human Rights (UDHR), facilitated the negotiations to secure consensus and chaired the principal three UN bodies, including the UN General Assembly that approved its final draft. Over half a century later and following an emerging discourse in the Arab world challenging human rights principles, a conference in Beirut, Lebanon (10–12 June 2003) sought to modify the Arab Charter on Human Rights (1994) towards a closer system to that of the UDHR (Chase and Hamzawy 2006). The Government of Lebanon has also endorsed and developed national roadmaps to achieve international targets set by the Millennium Development Goals (Abdul Samad 2003) and Sustainable Development Goals (El-Jisr and Chabarekh 2012). The Lebanese government has also facilitated the growth of a civil society and its thousands of non-governmental organizations (NGOs), including The Lebanese Transparency Association, Fighters for Peace, Association pour la Défense des Droits et des Libertés and the Lebanese Foundation for Permanent Civil Peace to uphold principles of human rights and foster sustainable peace.

Education has also taken seat in the front lines of attempts to foster active citizenship for social cohesion and democratic living. More specifically, citizenship education in Lebanon has been approached as a 'vehicle for social and civic reconstruction' (Frayha 2004, 174) and for 'minimizing the impact of sectarianism on the young generation' (Frayha 2003, 88). The design of citizenship education curricula stands on a foundation of nationalist ideologies that has also been the driving force for the three curricular reforms to date. As we shall see below, the visions of an ideal citizen, their identities and behaviours have largely shaped when, how and what education policy is written.

Education and curricular reforms

Citizenship education in the Lebanese national curriculum encompasses three subject areas: civics, history and geography. The programme that focuses most explicitly on citizenship is called *Al tarbiya al wataniya wa al tanshi'a al madaniyya*; although the official title translates into *National Education and Civic Training/Learning*, we can refer to it as *National and Civic Education* or civics. These three subjects have much in common. Frayha (1985) classifies them as social studies, using a more North American term when analysing the historical development of civics, history and geography for citizenship in Lebanon. Since the first national curriculum in 1946, the Government of Lebanon designed these three as mandatory subjects instructed across all four cycles. Each cycle comprises three grade levels, covering all 12 years of schooling. In the curricular timetable, each of these three subjects is taught 30 hours per school year, or 1 hour a week. Civics does stand out, however, as being the only subject in the national curriculum that has a textbook published by MEHE that all schools must use. Civics, geography and history are also the only three subjects (besides Arabic) that must be instructed and assessed only in Arabic. Official assessment by a government exam takes place after grade 9 for the Lebanese Baccalaureate I and after grade 12 for the Baccalaureate II.

The Lebanese programme of education has undergone three curricular reforms (1946, 1968–1971, 1997), each driven by a renewed ideal vision of citizenship. Across the reforms, education policy focused on strengthening a defined national identity, creating a sense of solidarity (among Lebanese, Arabs) and empowering young people to uphold principles of human rights and democracy when living in diversity. When Lebanon gained independence, the government wrote its first national curriculum in 1946, modifying the 1926 Ministère de l'Instruction Publique of the French mandate. It based education policy on the significance of transitioning from French governance to a sovereign nation-state. Aims of education strived to foster a nationalist Lebanese identity by demanding Arabic as the main language of study and nurturing patriotism through celebrated historical events, geographies and moral responsibilities towards Lebanese citizens and the country. The rise of pan-Arabism in the 1960s later triggered the second major curricular reform in 1968–1971. Indeed, Nasser's political Arab nationalist discourse spread across the entire region prompting education reforms. Frayha (2004) argued that the Arabization of the civics and history national curricula 'eliminated' Lebanese nationalism instituted by the 1946 curriculum (173). The significant emphasis of pan-Arabism over Lebanese nationalism further fuelled tensions between Lebanese nationalists and proponents of Arab nationalism.

The third and most up-to-date national curriculum resulted from the reforms that took place after the 15-year civil war. In September 1989, the members of parliament who survived the civil wars in Lebanon that erupted in 1975 met in Ta'if, Saudi Arabia, and formulated the peace treaty, The Document of National Accord. The Government of Lebanon signed the three-part blueprint for reconstruction into law in 1990. The third section of this peace agreement outlined five action points for education reform, the fifth stating: 'The curricula shall be reviewed and developed in a manner that strengthens national belonging, fusion, spiritual and cultural openness, and that unifies textbooks on the subjects of history and national education' (section III.F). The emphasis on unification of learning resource materials like textbooks was a response to the various history textbooks published by sectarian parties, which were perceived as weapons of war (Fontana 2017). In 1994, the Center for Educational Research and Development (CERD), an agency that supports the Lebanese MEHE through education research and curriculum development, carried out The Plan for Educational Reform, which resulted in a revised national curriculum (Ministry of Education and Higher Education [Lebanon] 1997). The history curriculum, however, was the only subject that caused controversy and did not pass reform legislature. The attempts to write a grand narrative and secure consensus among government officials failed in subsequent attempts (2000 and 2012), creating gridlock and an unchanged 1968–1971 history education curriculum.

The 1997 national curriculum, nevertheless, attempted to advance a vision of citizenship through principles of democracy, human rights, cosmopolitanism, peace and social cohesion. The Plan for Educational Reform aimed to ensure that the revised national curriculum would foster fundamental freedoms as human rights, openness to cultures around the world and a moral responsibility of all citizens to actively engage in society. Ironically, the *processes* of this curricular reform seemed to have undermined the democratic ideology of a post-armed conflict reformed Lebanese education system. BouJaoude and Ghaith (2006), for example, observed the absence of input from parents' and teachers' associations and students. Significant outcomes, however, include the declaration of a negotiated dual Lebanese and Arab national identity. The new vision also situated the citizen within the global community. More specific indicators of the ideal citizen are spelled out in the nine main aims of the *National and Civic Education* curriculum (Ministry of Education and Higher Education [Lebanon] 1997):

1. To prepare the student morally in harmony with the humanistic values in his [*sic*] community and country.
2. To introduce him [*sic*] to the vocational world and to build in him [*sic*] a spirit for work and appreciation for workers in different fields.
3. To prepare the student, in a civil sense, to enable him [*sic*] to contribute to world development in harmony with the spirit of modernity.
4. To teach how to critique, debate and to accept the other and to solve conflicts with his [*sic*] peers through a spirit of peace, justice and equality.
5. To build a social spirit so that he [*sic*] feels he [*sic*] is part of a larger community that is enriched with a diversity of ideas.
6. To raise the standards of his cultural, social, political and economic contributions and encourage his [*sic*] free participation in his [*sic*] civil life.
7. To promote his [*sic*] devotion/loyalty to his [*sic*] Lebanese identity, land and country through a cohesive and unifying democratic framework.
8. To raise the awareness of his [*sic*] Arab identity and his [*sic*] loyalty to it and a sense of Arab belonging to it that is open to the whole world.
9. To promote the awareness of his [*sic*] humanity through the close relationships with his [*sic*] fellow man [*sic*] regardless of gender, colour, religion, language, culture and any other differences.[1]

These nine aims appear to embrace multiple levels of identities, uphold human rights principles and demand critical and active participation. In addition to promoting the dual Lebanese and Arab nationalist identities, other aims make direct reference to global and cosmopolitan forms of citizenship. As global citizens, they would contribute to world development (aim 3) and express a sense of openness to the whole world (aim 8). Young people would also develop a cosmopolitan dimension to citizenship by championing moral responsibilities that reflect on humanistic principles (aim 1) and identifying oneself as a human being within a larger community of other human beings as unconditional equals (aim 9). The language, however, is in the male tense and, thus, reflects an implicit gendered view of citizenship.

---

[1] The translation of these nine main aims of civic education in the Lebanese national curriculum also appears in Akar (2012, 470–80).

After 70 years of compulsory citizenship education

Research on the Lebanese formal educational programme for citizenship, namely civics, mostly includes critical analyses of curricular content and socio-political agendas. In a comprehensive investigation of the historical development of citizenship education in Lebanon from the Ottoman rule until the second curricular reform of 1968–1971, Frayha (1985) analysed how political transformations including independence and pan-Arabism had policymakers translated Lebanese and Arab nationalisms into education policy, including the emphasis of Arabic instruction and patriotism. Decades later, a surge of citizenship education research critically reviewed the third national curriculum in 1997, focusing mostly on discourse analysis of civics curricular aims and textbooks.

In an initial content analysis examining the 1997 civics curriculum and textbooks, Zoreik (2000) found that the aims and presentation of information suggested teacher-centred learning activities such as dictating lessons, many of which reinforced gender stereotypes. Soon after, the Lebanese Association for Educational Studies (LAES) published a volume series critically reviewing the various subject programmes of the national curriculum. The LAES commissioned Adonis Acra to identify strengths and weaknesses in the civics curricula's rationale, aims, educational approaches, scope, sequence, content and terminology. The civics curricular discourse reflected commitments to democracy, human rights, civil peace, active participation, dialogue and openness but seemed to have left out wider concepts of peace and multiple perspectivism and saturated the programme with information, leaving little room to critically engage and reflect (LAES 2003). In a subsequent vision document intended to outline a national education strategy, the LAES (2006) expressed further concerns over the civics curriculum's poor alignment between its curricular aims and specific learning objectives.

In 2013, UNICEF commissioned the Centre for Lebanese Studies to examine the extent to which civics textbooks cover human rights, gender-related issues, conflict management and dialogue. The findings, published in Shuayb (2015), showed that human rights are sporadic, though present, across the four cycles; the textbooks make no reference to children's rights, comprise only one unit on human rights and the only category listed is citizen's rights. The study also found that the textbooks almost completely dismiss addressing gender-based violence and, instead, reinforce socially constructed gender roles such as females managing the household while males carry out professional positions. While conflict management and dialogue are explicitly stated in one of the nine general aims of civic education, they appear in a grade 8 lesson on family and grade 10 unit on conflict as concepts defined by causes and examples of conflict and a broad view of best practices of managing conflict and engaging in dialogue. Moreover, the textbooks give no opportunities to reflect on personal experiences or engage in dialogic or conflict management activities. These findings were consistent with other studies that described the textbooks as documents of information for young people to memorize (LAES 2007), idealistic with no references to current events or issues (LAES 2003), and filled with theories that lack opportunities to explore through learning activities (Al-Habbal 2011; Shuayb 2007; Zoreik 2000).

Studies have also started to explore learning and instruction in the civics classroom. By adopting the 1999 CivEd instrument, the Government of Lebanon and the UNDP tested 3111 grade-9 students' civic knowledge, attitudes and values and administered questionnaires to 111 school principals and 191 civic education teachers. Responses related to pedagogy revealed that learning activities mostly involved memorizing information to later recite for assessment with almost no opportunities to engage in discussions, research or exploring different views (UNDP, MEHE and CDR 2008). Teachers' responses also suggested that they were confident in their traditional approaches to instruction and, thus, preferred neither to discuss choice of topics with students nor how to learn the material. Other small-scale studies consistently arrived at similar conclusions. Shuayb (2007) administered questionnaires across a range of schools in Lebanon and found that 77.7 per cent of teachers believed that 'Students are here to learn what the teacher knows' and 74.8 per cent agreed that 'I teach students the way I want and believe without listening to their views'. In a small-scale study (Jabbour 2014), a close-ended questionnaire showed that 100 per cent of the seventy secondary school student participants agreed that memorizing information is the best way to get a good grade and the teachers (a) mostly lecture while students listen, (b) ask questions and students answer and (c) lecture material from the civics textbook.

Empirical studies exploring citizenship education policy and practice have shown a dominant pedagogical culture of memorizing information, which counters the human rights and democratic principles of accessing information and freedom of expression. However, learning about the relations between the rhetoric of education policy and realities of teaching and learning citizenship in schools has mostly employed quantitative methods of enquiry. Close-ended questionnaires facilitated the collection and analysis of information from large samples of schools across the country. However, I have argued (Akar 2017a) that the use of quantitative approaches for these initial explorations into understandings of citizenship and experiences of learning and teaching inside the civics classroom yields two main shortcomings. The first is drawn from the ontological assumption that certain concepts of citizenship are universal in nature. The two large-scale studies on citizenship education in Lebanon – UNDP, MEHE and CDR (2008) and Shuayb (2007) – relied mostly on indicators defining concepts of democratic citizenship and social cohesion, respectively, in Western Europe and North America. Indeed, Edward Said (1978) forewarned against the imperial-driven ontologies that shape knowledge production in different cultures around the world. The second limitation comes from the epistemological approach of administering close-ended questions to learn about individual conceptualizations of socially constructed phenomena like citizenship. Quantitative-based studies on citizenship and citizenship education have overlooked students' and teachers' individual understandings and experiences of citizenship and their reflections on learning and teaching (Hahn 2010; Kennedy 2007; Rubin 2007). Hence, the large-scale international [and national] quantitative-based studies on citizenship and citizenship education have mostly measured teachers' and students' 'understandings of *others*' understandings of citizenship' (Akar 2017a, 3).

The next two chapters present results from open-ended survey packs and classroom discussions with students and semi-structured interviews with civics teachers in Lebanon. The survey packs were designed as open-ended learning activities that gave young people an opportunity to describe their understandings and experiences of being good citizens and discuss their learning experiences in the civics classroom. Engaging young people in these reflective and critical dialogues that also empower them to put into practice their human right to participate in decisions that concern them (United Nations 1989, article 12) constitutes a pedagogical research process (Starkey et al. 2014). The findings build a growing empirical field of individual conceptualizations and narratives that show the extent to which formal education fosters and undermines a citizenship for living together in areas affected by conflict.

5

Young People: Their Citizenship, Their Learning

Hundreds of Lebanese young people in secondary schools in Lebanon wrote and talked about activities *they* considered as characteristic of good citizens and reflected on their learning experiences in the civics classroom. Then, they prioritized nine themes illustrating maximal and minimal notions of citizenship through a diamond-nine ranking exercise (see Table 5.1). For the final written activity, they described their learning experiences inside the civics classroom and then drew on these during the class discussion at the end. Their narratives of good citizenship showed degrees of empowerment and engagement for a communitarian concept of citizenship, one that mostly sought after the welfare of the community and individuals in need. Although their descriptions of citizenship reflected many of the principles of human rights, democracy and social cohesion portrayed in the national curriculum, they attributed most of their conceptualizations of citizenship to experiences outside the formal school setting. Indeed, their learning experiences in the classroom appeared to foster a passive or even submissive form of citizenship that they vehemently challenged. Instead, spaces like their community, civil society, homes and role models had

Table 5.1 Nine themes of citizenship for ranking

Voting in elections	Debating with others	Knowing the history
Protecting the environment	Singing the national anthem	Knowing good manners
Knowing your human rights	Volunteering or helping others	Knowing the laws

This chapter is derived, in part, from an article published in *British Journal of Sociology of Education*, volume 37, on 28 July 2014, available at: https://doi.org/10.1080/01425692.2014.916603.

provided them with the opportunities to engage and reflect as active citizens living in diversity and an area affected by conflict.

Young people's narratives of conceptualizing citizenship

Their narratives of good citizenship were drawn from personal experiences and aspirations. From a total of 2,178 open-ended responses, almost half reflected on actions related to rights and responsibilities across a range of communities, over a third expressed concerns for individuals in need and a fifth explained how self-development and personal achievements were forms of good citizenship. They also reflected on a role model they considered to be an ideal citizen, which yielded similar descriptions of good citizenship to their own. After completing the diamond ranking, they wrote justifications for the first and last ranks, which gave even greater insight to their conceptualizations of citizenship.

Personal experiences and aspirations

Almost half the total descriptions of good citizenship they believed they had exercised and wish to carry out some day related to helping individuals in need, including friends, family, elderly, orphans and disabled people. Many wrote about giving advice to friends about personal issues and helping family members at home, for example, with chores. They also frequently mentioned times they had helped the poor by donating money, food or clothes; 'visited a nursing home and got [the elderly] gifts'; 'cooked for orphans'; and visited or volunteered at a children's cancer centre. While some expressed desires to help poor people by building homes, end child labour, opening 'a free school' and becoming a doctor to help those 'who can't afford medication', far more focused on supporting orphaned children by wanting to 'open an organization', 'make a home shelter' and 'get more kids adopted'. The ideas of working in civil society or building a space that provides a social service were quite common. Other examples included helping children with cancer by 'be[ing] part of an NGO' or children in poverty by 'open[ing] a place on my money with free food for children'. The only references made outside the Lebanese context were two: helping disabled people in Lourdes and children in Africa.

Many also reflected on their degrees of participation during and after the Israeli offensive in 2006, which took place almost a year prior to data collection. Responses concerning war victims were also related primarily to activities in their local geography. For example, half the responses concerning war victims came from students in South Lebanon saying how they stayed and helped the civil defence and other organizations. They recalled that they had 'helped refugees' by 'giving food' and 'helped pick up dead bodies of children during the war'. After the war, many young people still participated through organizations and supported 'the people that come to Lebanon to dismantle the landmines' by helping organize and contributing to fundraisers. In other regions like North Lebanon, Beirut and Mount Lebanon, they 'helped refugees' or 'people who left South Lebanon during the war' by joining organizations, volunteering or 'receiving refugees from the war in my house'.

Over a third of all the responses prioritized rights and responsibilities across communities like the natural environment, civil society, the nation-state, the political sphere and their own that are characterized by diversity and differences. Most frequently, the students made reference to the natural environment by recalling projects they had participated in, like 'cleaning beaches' or 'planting Lebanon with trees'. They noted that these cleaning campaigns that they had participated in were organized by various organizations such as an environmental NGO, scouts, the municipality or their school. Less than a handful mentioned recycling while a third expressed minimal behaviours such as 'I don't throw garbage on the street' or 'by avoiding throwing things on the ground'. Yet, concerns for sustainability were focused primarily on Lebanon's mountains, sea and streets as well as 'my village' and 'my neighbourhood'.

While dozens wrote about their previous work with NGOs, even more expressed aspirations of continuing their work in civil society and even establishing their own organization. The Red Cross seemed to have been the most popular of NGOs as a space to volunteer or donate; some 'attended a few courses at the Lebanese Red Cross' or 'helped the Red Cross'. The degrees of commitment expressed by so many young people suggest a certain Red Cross phenomenon. Another popular organization was one concerning human rights. Actually, all those who made some reference to a human rights organization came from young people in South Lebanon who reported they had joined one through either their school or community. Also, from South Lebanon, young people aspired to establish 'an organization to make people aware and to protect the environment from danger', 'an organization against sectarianism' and 'an organization to boycott American and Israeli products'. Young people in other parts of the country expressed desires of establishing centres that provides social services for free, such as a school, hospital, orphanage, 'care centers', 'a library' or recreational facilities for youth. Some further explained their commitments to NGOs by describing civil society as a space that 'benefits the community' and 'brings me closer to society'.

Direct references to the country were less frequent, but still illustrated struggles within a site affected by conflict. Less than a dozen reported on moments they assisted in development activities by 'defending my country' or 'defending my community'. However, themes of reconstruction emerged in over sixty responses claiming they want to 'help maintain the unity of the people of the country', 'make the streets clean', 'repair some of the roads', 'improve my country's economy' and making 'Lebanon be a much better place' while others expressed desires to defend or fight for the country 'against the enemy' or 'prevent anything bad that Arabs are influenced with from overseas'. National pride also emerged by addressing current issues in Lebanon like emigration, 'I make people who don't love to study here love to study by giving them the positive side of Lebanon'. Some also highlighted the negative image of Lebanon through the international mass media and, thus, wanted to 'get politically involved to alter certain harsh views about Lebanon' because 'all propaganda around [portrays] us [as] terrorists and [that] we have no civilization while we do'. Others turned to tourism by 'welcoming guests' from overseas and having them 'feel at home'.

Within the political sphere, we see a split between those who find it a critical space for change and those who associate it with roots of conflict. A large group from the former recalled when they 'marched in a walk to help promote peace' and that the 'demonstration has made me feel a sense of belonging'. A smaller group wrote about activities from their political party where they were able to 'express my political opinion through sharing some of the Lebanese opposition activities' and 'support the Lebanese resistance against Israel'. Nearly two dozen found it important to participate in political parties, another group aspired to be politicians, one wanted to make new laws and one would 'like to go to every minister and president and talk about my feelings toward this life that is full of problems and ask them many questions and the first question is "Why are you here?" and "What are you doing here?"'

However, a few students preferred 'not to interfere in politics' for 'in order to make friends' because 'political parties … usually causes problems'. While some also mentioned that talking about religion brings out similar problems, another group of students believed that being part of a 'religious club', 'always follow my religion' and even to build a church or mosque contributed to their concepts of good citizenship. While desires to participate as members of parliament and other forms of political involvement came from all regions, more specific types of political affairs seemed to be influenced by activities in their locales. For instance, more students in Beirut than other places wrote about participating in demonstrations while more from the North and Mount Lebanon showed greater interests in political parties. Also, those in South Lebanon reflected more on the resistance against Israel while students from other provinces focused on national unity.

Students also identified people with diverse backgrounds as a community in itself and emphasized the importance of communication for living together. They believed that they had behaved as good citizens by 'being polite and respectable', trying to 'communicate with others in a productive way', treating each other fairly and maintaining relationships. Some had focused on dialogue and communication by wanting 'to listen carefully to other people's opinions' and being calmer. Others made several references to social interactions such as 'behaving well with people' and working and interacting 'with other citizens which will make my country prosper and grow'. Many also addressed conflicts among people and explained how they have either 'helped solve some arguments' or resolved 'a struggle between two friends'. Descriptions of resolving conflicts were also presented as ongoing struggles as they wanted to continue 'fighting corruption', 'stop the killings in Lebanon', and 'try to explain to the Arabic community that there needs to be some equality between a man and a woman'. Gender equality emerged also as a right that needed fighting for, mostly for 'giving women their complete rights' and 'change society's views towards women' but was mentioned by only fifteen students and only one being a male. Although very few reflected on the notion of human rights, those who did recalled times they practised their rights such as expressing their opinions when 'working in the press club of my school' or 'speak my words as a Lebanese'.

A minority of students explained how they perceive their personal achievements and developments as important aspects of good citizenship. Most important was 'being educated', 'getting good grades' and passing the government exams because 'being successful in school … makes me an important person in society' and even 'represent' the country better. Many also felt that continuing through to higher education or 'keeping learning things' like the history of Lebanon, other languages, sciences and law would enable them to become better citizens. Even through the arts, some felt that they could contribute to their community by playing music, dancing and 'keep on with my writings and trying to make a change'. For some, having a summer job had brought them closer to their community while getting a 'good job' in the future for personal wealth, success and self-worth 'would make me feel like a useful citizen' or 'would make my nation proud', especially if the work was 'in my own country, not somewhere else'. Many also attributed personality traits and morality to informed decisions and behaviours of good citizenship. For instance, one reflected on how 'I've taught myself how to control my temper' and another on 'knowing bad from good and having limits'. Other statements related a wide range of traits to good citizenship, including open-mindedness, assertiveness, self-confidence, independence, responsibility, composure and persistence. Moreover, a few described how they developed these traits through their involvement in music and writing.

Role models

Young people also wrote about a role model they had regarded as an ideal citizen. The vast majority described individuals who contributed towards either reconstruction after the civil war or liberation from occupation. After the civil war, model citizens 'rebuilt and reconstructed Lebanon' by 'build[ing] bridges and modern buildings', improving the economy and promoting tourism. Those who defended the country had 'liberated Lebanon from Israeli occupation' by 'fighting the enemy to achieve liberty' or by being 'in the army and services the country'. There were no significant differences across the variables of religious denomination and province. Less revolutionary figures still exhibited democratic behaviours like 'following all the rules and paying taxes', 'practicing their rights and abiding by the law' or just trying to lead a 'peaceful and successful life'. Others described model citizens who celebrated national symbols and sentiments where they 'glorified the country through nationalistic songs', 'always do parties for the village' or even 'not leaving their society'. Similar role models were described because they promoted Lebanon within the global community through sports, music, career or diplomacy and international relations in order 'to make the world to see Arabs better'. In contrast to celebrating patriotism, some mentioned individuals who contributed to science such as one who 'put a lot of formulas in physics and helped us live a new technological world' and another researching a 'cure for cancer'. Very few wrote about non-Lebanese people; those mentioned had 'boycott[ed] salt from the British in India' and 'encourages all countries to unite (America, Arabia, European)'. Some had cleverly characterized nearly all role models mentioned as citizens who 'went beyond personal benefits to help his [*sic*] community and country' and who 'sacrificed many things they like to do for the benefit of others'.

Another group of young people wrote about role models who helped people in need, mainly through financial assistance or voluntary service. Some reportedly covered students' tuition fees for higher education or medical bills by 'donat[ing] money to people with cancer' and 'provid[ing] medicine to those who couldn't afford it'. Model citizens were also those who 'rebuilt houses' for those destroyed in the 2006 Israeli war or volunteered to help the elderly, poor, orphaned, blind and victims of the war by setting up organizations and 'not charge people when treated them'. While the majority of role models were those who provided for their 'homeland people', meaning Lebanon, others were from around the world who fought for human rights. Some cited those who struggled against segregation and racism of African Americans, tried to reduce poverty in Africa, 'helped the families who survived the hurricanes', 'adopting children from poor countries' and mentioned the individual who founded the Red Cross 'during his travel from Switzerland to Italy and helped injured people'.

Finally, they described the knowledge fields that they believe enabled their role models to engage as ideal citizens. At one level, they referred to knowledge related to profession such as studying medicine, technology, teaching, first-aid and 'how to use the Braille typing machine'. A few focused on financial success and appreciated 'the technique of earning money fast in order to use it in helping others'. Slightly more specific actions were associated with defending the nation through 'skills in fighting and defending', 'war strategy', 'how to use weapons' and understanding the enemy. Nearly all the model citizens were attributed with the knowledge of being 'an active member and not a parasite' in order to make the community 'a better place to live'. Some of these actions suggested violence through armed resistance against oppressors because 'no revolution can be made without guns' or breaking the law 'because he knew he's doing the right thing'. Contrary to violent forms of action aimed at treating 'people from different religions ... equally' or trying to 'unite all people excluding the differences between them'. Such actions required knowing how to communicate with others through 'diplomacy', 'preaching', 'public speaking', 'patience' and 'debate'. However, maintaining integrity was still important to one whose model citizen refused to 'kiss the asses of politicians'.

Most young people described their role models through psychology, more specifically, personality traits and abilities to manage emotions. They quite frequently wrote terms related to courage, sensitivity, generosity, 'not having pride', self-confidence and compassion. Showing compassion meant that their model citizens would 'feel pain for one's country', know 'the feeling of poor people; the way they live', respect 'the feelings of people they are working with' and 'put himself in the shoes of others'. One believed that experiencing struggles had fostered compassion to help 'a lot of people because he [has] tasted the bitterness of life and knows that if he helped someone he might erase that bitterness'. Many also illustrated sacrifice as an action of empathy and generosity. They describe how their model citizens had sacrificed money, time and even their lives when helping others and the community. Moreover, those who have put their 'own life on the line' have passed on 'blood [as] a debt … to continue as they went'. Finally, some appreciated feelings of 'love and unity' and believed they mostly resulted from being parents and raising a family.

Their notions of citizenship: Maximal, minimal and communitarian

Young people in Lebanon expressed what they have conceptualized as maximal and minimal notions of citizenship, including indications of communitarianism. Based on their reported experiences and observations, a minority suggested a minimal or even passive notion of citizenship. Virtually all males, for example, did not mention any gender-based issues when describing conflicts or injustices. The single community they gave most attention to was the nation-state. Even when making reference to the international community, they expressed concerns over the global reputation of Lebanon. Nevertheless, mentions of Lebanon were contextualized along with the natural environment and people in need, regardless of their political or religious identities. Clearly, there was a high regard for the wider human community when they described experiences and aspirations of supporting the disadvantaged and working with or organizing their own NGO. Very few, actually, reflected on issues beyond Lebanon's political borders; but when they did, they expressed concern over the welfare of the Arab region and people suffering in other parts of the world. Interestingly, nobody really expressed some form of unconditional commitment exclusively to one community, such as a political party or a religious sect. Other elements of citizenship that suggested basic or minimal forms of participation came from some responses that stated law-abiding practices like not littering or paying taxes.

While the above indications of minimal notions of citizenship emerged from interpretations of their reports on good citizenship, young people's explicit explanations of what they viewed as passive came from the diamond ranking exercise. Almost two-thirds of the students placed *voting in elections* and *singing the national anthem* in one of the last three spots. While some of those who placed *singing the national anthem* as least important perceived it as an 'expression of your respect towards your country', they still regarded it as a passive and ineffective practice of good citizenship because 'you're not contributing anything to the country' and '[it] won't save lives or fix anything'. To further explain, some gave examples of more effective 'actions [that] proves his nationality' such as 'by working, studying and uniting and not by saying the anthem'. Others explained that 'citizenship is an inner quality not something we spell' and 'the love of one's country is not through the national anthem but through sacrifice and respect for the laws'. Voting in elections, however, is a democratic practice and right that gives people voice to elect representatives in government. However, the vast majority associated elections with politics and the Lebanese government system, which they argued 'only makes people fight', 'is destroying the country' and, thus, are roots to 'all the conflicts' in Lebanon. Some described politicians as 'all a bunch of liars', 'the reason for wars' and 'pretend to be caring and helpful to others'. Some of these views were also used to justify open-ended responses that explained why avoiding politics was a practice of good citizenship.

The self-reports of young people illustrate various degrees of engagement and empowerment as well as levels of identities they mostly relate with. They seemed to be informed and concerned about current issues like emigration, threats to the natural environment, security, corruption and human rights violations. They addressed issues at numerous levels of communities, including national (reducing youth emigration to build Lebanon); social (improving women's rights, medical care and access to education); environmental (protecting nature); political (avoiding or participating in politics); and, though to a much lesser extent, global levels (improving Lebanon's international reputation and welfare of children in Africa). Probably the most immediate community was family and friends whom they reported to have helped and wanted to make proud. Many also believed that close ties towards family members nurture an element of care that enables people to help others. Indeed, this was demonstrated in the significant increase of responses towards reconstruction and development in the country as activities they would like to be involved in from the significant number of examples of good citizenship behaviours they reported to have already carried out towards family and friends.

Nearly all appeared to have shown a degree of connection to people in need. They described this community as comprising human beings who have been marginalized and made vulnerable by old age, poverty, terminal illness, armed conflict and loss of parents. The various forms of practices towards people in need ranged across degrees of engagement from donating money, food or clothes and visiting residential care facilities to cooking and volunteering.

However, evidence of having organized or led a campaign or community project did not really emerge. Nevertheless, despite contentions towards government institutions and politics, many still seemed committed to change through the political and public spheres, mostly civil society. The majority exhibited a sense of empowerment to provide social services by establishing their own organizations or building centres like schools or hospitals. Some even critically challenged politicians and showed some interest in creating new laws.

These findings suggest a youth that is largely not apathetic. They illustrated a citizenry that extends over and above the obligations set by civil laws. Through their narratives, they presented themselves as individuals who bring to classrooms a momentum of concerns about injustices and confidence in their agency that they conceptualized by critically reflecting on their experiences and observations. Moreover, they appear to have found civil society as a public sphere of hope and opportunities. Maximal and active notions of citizenship could be expected among young people in areas affected by conflict. In a large-scale quantitative study on civic competence of 14-year-olds in Europe, Hoskins et al. (2008) found participatory attitudes were highest in Cyprus, Portugal, Romania, Poland and Slovakia while Sweden, Finland, Germany, Switzerland and England scored the lowest. And for citizenship values, Romania, Lithuania, Cyprus and Poland had high scores while Finland, Belgium (French-speaking) and England scored the lowest. The evidence suggested that young people from countries in northern and western parts of Europe may have scored lower than others because their democracies were more stable and longer-established, while those from southern and eastern regions of Europe that experience lesser stability could 'have a greater intention to participate in order to develop and maintain it in their country' (Hoskins et al. 2008, 63). Not all young people in areas of conflict, however, conceptualize maximal notions of citizenship. Many become habituated to life conditions under oppressive regimes as we have seen most recently through the era of political revolutions in the Arab region. In Lebanon, democratic discourses at home, in the media and other cultural venues prevent, to some degree, the normalization of corruption, gender-based violence and other forms of conflict, sustaining desires and struggles for social justice.

If citizenship, in its broadest sense, is the relationship between the individual and the community, then these young people have identified themselves with communities of people in need and the welfare of the nation-state and natural environment. These indications of a communitarian construct of citizenship can be expected in a political culture that embraces nationalist ideologies to foster collective identities and memories (Beiner 1995). Among their attributes of communitarianism, they made frequent references to *sacrifice* of time, money or even life; *benevolence* through compassion and care; *solidarity* to unify for social justice; and the value *kinship* and other close family-like relationships. Solidarity and kinship, however, could potentially undermine principles of equality and inclusion if they are isolated from mechanisms that safeguard against nepotism and other forms of corruption and exclusive participation in the public sphere.

Sites and experiences of conceptualizing citizenship

Young people's narratives suggest that their conceptualizations of good citizenship had been largely shaped by extra-curricular activities at school, events taken place in their local region, civil society and, to a lesser degree, role models. When schools secure funding for transportation and feel safe taking children to visit sites off campus, they commonly organize excursions to nature spots, museums or residential care facilities for orphans or the elderly. These visits – or even when NGOs visit schools to collect donations or distribute material/information – could have quite likely drawn associations between good citizenship on the one hand and orphans or the elderly as individuals in need and provisions made through civil society on the other. For probably all the activities, it was difficult to see if these young people had been active in identifying, planning and implementing or merely participated in activities organized for them. Considering their reflections on learning civics later on in this chapter, it is very unlikely that their classroom experiences had any influence on their constructs of good citizenship.

In addition to school, their narratives suggested that local events also shaped their constructs of good citizenship. For example, students mostly from North and Mount Lebanon described giving shelter to internally displaced people from the Israeli offensive on Lebanese territory in 2006. Participating in demonstrations most frequently came from young people in Beirut, the capital and a focal point for social movements and protests. Mostly students from South Lebanon wrote about supporting NGOs for human rights and wanting to volunteer with the Civil Defense, a government emergency unit for fire, rescue and ambulance. The South Lebanon governorate is extremely vulnerable to conflict, especially since Israel occupied a swath of territory in South Lebanon and battles with Hezbollah forces who are stationed in South Lebanon. Moreover, Lebanon is currently in a state of war with Israel. This could also explain why narratives on defending the country came almost entirely from students in the south. Also, the young peoples' descriptions of their model citizens reflected many of the identities, values and behaviours in their narratives of personal experiences.

Across the schools and regions, civil society and NGOs had probably the greatest impact in young peoples' conceptualizations of good citizenship. The students expressed desires to work within civil society nearly three times more than those who had participated in NGO-related activities, all for the purpose of helping those in need or further developing the country. However, we can raise questions when less than 1 per cent mentioned actively participating in the political or government system, including being a mayor and one wanted to change the constitution. An active and well-funded civil society is critical for a nation-state's progress and development, especially when the government institutions are weakened by armed conflicts and other forms of instability. Lebanon's diversity of destructive conflicts has drawn in thousands of NGOs, many of them as international organizations. Their activities for development range across a variety of sectors, including environment, education, democracy, re-construction and health. The students in this study named several of these NGOs: Future Youth, Caritas, Model UN, Mosan, Greenpeace and the Red Cross. The Red Cross, probably the largest running NGO in Lebanon and the official emergency medical service provider, has generated a culture of collaboration, collegiality and voluntary service among the youth in Lebanon. As a university student in Beirut, my friends would reminisce the days they used to skip classes in secondary school to hang out and volunteer at the Red Cross.

Indeed, government sector representatives have expressed their support for and even reliance on civil society for social reconstruction and other forms of development. However, activities organized by NGOs that overlook approaches and opportunities to participate in and through government institutions risk marginalizing students from government systems. Moreover, the pedagogical experiences of formal civic education suggest that young people may be learning to distance themselves from government institutions and live as active citizens within the public sphere generated by civil society. I explore this further in Chapter 7.

Young people's model of citizenship education

The rankings of the nine main themes and the written justifications unexpectedly suggested an educational model to learning citizenship. Their model comprises three dimensions to learning citizenship: universal principles, knowledge of communities and active participation. Moreover, its agreement with related literature even demonstrates a degree of validity. Nearly two-thirds of the students placed *knowing good manners* in the top region. Their written justifications explained that any form of engagement must first be grounded in a set of core values or principles. They suggested a normative set of principles that includes politeness, respect, benevolence, kinship, sacrifice, solidarity and civility. The concept of defining values to underpin ideal notions of democratic citizenship has also been argued in the form of presuppositions (Crick 2000), procedural values (Parekh 2000) and virtues of citizenship (Kymlicka 2001). Presuppositions or universalistic principles outlined in the literature above include respecting differences, fairness, equality and non-violent communication. In addition, Starkey (1992) argues how human rights principles are found in western European, North American and Islamic traditions and define basic, universal values for peace and justice.

Students then suggested, through their comments near the first and last themes of the diamond ranking, that the knowledge of human rights and laws precedes activities of active participation such as *protecting the environment, debating with others* and *volunteering or helping others*. They argued that the knowledge of rights and laws provide people with the confidence and security of having freedoms and rights and foster a sense of commitment to rules so people would know what they can and cannot do. For example, human rights education defines various forms of freedoms that all people are entitled to and that also serve as guiding principles for active participation. Parker (2004) and Walter and MacLeod (2002) maintain a similar argument showing how principles and knowledge of communities mostly determine how we behave or participate as citizens. Parker (2004) argues that engagement is shaped by bodies of knowledge (e.g. understandings, skills and principles) and the absence of universal principles (e.g. human rights) and knowledge of social studies can generate forms of engagement that threaten peace and justice, as demonstrated by the Ku Klux Klan and al-Qaeda. Even Arab literature on citizenship suggests that political leadership requires a strong foundation of disciplinary knowledge, such as history (Khalidi 1992). Therefore, the knowledge-participation relationship informs 'enlightened political engagement' where knowledge and active participation educate individuals to walk the 'democratic path in a diverse society' (Parker 2003, 33).

The students' indications of a model of citizenship education for active citizenship suggest that we can best learn to be active citizens when we first establish a set of universal principles. What they considered as normative –

respect, solidarity, sacrifice, civility – would then underpin the learning of content knowledge and the practices of dialogue and active participation. According to their written justifications, learning human rights and laws would spell out the freedoms and limitations of participation and even establish common ground among individuals from different backgrounds. Active participation would, therefore, inform and be informed by the humanistic and democratic principles and learnings of rights, obligations and social studies like history, sociology and political science.

Learning experiences in the civics classroom

Hundreds of young people across Lebanon wrote about classroom experiences they considered as learning opportunities and found difficult and listed suggestions to improve the civics classroom. They appreciated curricular topics related to their daily lives and activities that involved dialogue and participation as essential and enjoyable to their citizenship learning. However, they expressed resistance to memorization and feelings of demotivation from the lessons in the textbook which came as prescriptive and hypocritical.

Opportunities of learning citizenship

The majority first appreciated learning about topics like families, the United Nations and the Arab League, community service, laws, human rights, poverty, pollution, voting and elections, adolescents, conflict and dialogue, political parties and the resistance. Over half said they found them relevant and practical to daily life. For example, lessons on adolescents 'give advices' and address topics 'we are really living in and know about them'. Lessons on family were 'so close to how we live' and 'one day I'm gonna have a family and I'm gonna use these things'. Lessons on dialogue and conflict resolution were also listed as relevant because 'every day we confront conflicts that need to be resolved' and learning how to 'debate … helps a lot in life in order to avoid problems like talking and interruption so we would know how to talk and debate in life'. Several students recalled the lesson on voting and elections 'since we can express our voice' and because elections 'is most important for democracy to be applied'. Some also believed that by learning about poverty, pollution, human rights violations and corruption, 'we gave them importance'; and by doing so, 'the conflicts would disappear and peace would prevail'. Their reasons for selecting the topics also revealed a great deal about what communities they related to and how. Many reported they enjoyed learning about political parties 'since we have a variety of them' and some appreciated the lesson on the 'protection of the country'. At regional and global levels, many students found the Arab–Israeli conflict most enjoyable 'because it resembles the conflict we are living and it shows the injustice that is happening and how powerful countries don't have a commitment to human rights'. A more global-related topic was the lesson on pollution 'because it's an important issue everywhere and it could lead to major changes in our world'.

Less than a fifth recalled participating in learning activities inside the classroom. They mentioned in-class discussions, debates, mock elections and role play because 'all the class shared in'. The most popular were dialogic activities like in-class discussions because issues were 'expressed with your own words' and, during debates, 'we were able to give our opinions freely'. One common topic of debate was on political parties where students researched political parties and in class 'we had a dialogue, us and the teacher, and we saw all the political directions of all the class members'. One student wrote:

> I loved the lesson in civics about the political parties. It was special because it wasn't an ordinary lesson like the teacher talking and the students taking notes and sleeping, but on the contrary, we discussed the matter. Each student specified to what political regime he/she belonged and why. It was nice to know how every person thinks.

These testimonies, however, seemed to be the exception. Some years later, when I had the opportunity to visit classrooms, I observed that talk in the classroom was mostly in the form of rhetorical dialogues, driven by teachers' close-ended questions searching for responses evaluated as correct or incorrect (Akar 2016). Indeed, dialogic and participative activities were apparently facilitated merely as short-lived demonstrations. Another example is observed in lessons on elections. A few reflected on having in-class elections for their lesson on voting and democracy when 'we brought a box and we voted on a certain topic' because 'we got a taste of real-life voting'. Such activities, however, had simulated elections rather than integrated them as some form of common practice to actually experience as a form of living.

Finally, many wrote about the collegial and collaborative dynamics in the classroom among themselves and their teacher and how the social and emotional experiences had made an impact on their learning. During one of the class discussions, one group recalled a time when the teacher had staged a conflict with one of the students, 'As the teacher and the other student were arguing and us watching we learned more about conflicts: how they start and what happens during and after the conflict'. They highlighted the powerful experiences of 'cooperation between us and the teacher'. Another class bragged about their opportunities to collaborate with each other and found that 'my classmates made it simple, easy to understand' and valued civics as a class where 'not only the teacher is the one who teaches but the students can participate and discuss many issues'. More observable emotions like cheerfulness and sorrow were also associated with positive, memorable learning experiences. Many remembered times they had laughed in class and believed that their teachers' sense of humour helped them learn. Interestingly, the political philosopher Wingo (2006) argues for the consideration of laughter or '*viwir* – a civic form of joy and laughter' is an essential element for 'human well-being and democracy' (202). Certain topics addressing social injustices and nationalism emotionally moved the learners. Slavery and gender inequalities, for example, 'affected me a lot so I cried'. Other topics like defending the country and the resistance 'touch you from the inside' and 'all the class members were united, and it's the first time'. The dynamics shaped by humour and vulnerability illustrated a rather flat hierarchy in the classroom, which they associated with trust and learning. However, these incidents emerged more of the exception according to their reports and especially the following subsection on difficulties of learning citizenship.

Difficult learning experiences

Almost all wrote about difficult moments in learning civics. The high frequency of narratives and examples of challenges focused mostly on actual learning experiences in the classroom with very little mention of topics. Topics that did emerge, however, included studying government institutions such as law, the constitution, judicial system and systems of government, but were mentioned in association with practices of memorization. Although less than a handful reported they enjoyed civics for being 'easy to memorize', over 200 voiced their concerns of learning to recite information for assessment. Indeed, memorization was the dominant pedagogy. They used the terms studying, memorizing and rote learning interchangeably and contrasted them with 'understanding'. For instance, 'it's hard for me to study the lessons by heart'; 'studying word by word the lesson (law)'; and 'studying is the most difficult thing in civics class because we have to memorize and not understand'. They also argued how memorization hindered their learning because they were 'going to forget it after three minutes'.

One strongly believed that 'as long as we're forced to memorize, we will not learn the REAL meaning of civics because then civics will just be a subject that we study for grades and not for discussion and experience'. Thus, in addition to finding difficulties in the actual skill of memorizing, many found that it contradicts their understandings of the nature of citizenship – an active and participative practice.

A large number expressed a lack of motivation or even a form of resistance to learning civics. They argued and suggested that information was presented in its ideal form with neither references to nor opportunity to explore the injustices around them such as human rights violations, corruption and the social injustice of work opportunities being mostly accessible to those with connections. They illustrated a sense of hypocrisy when 'civics lessons talk about the rules in our community but the rules aren't followed anyway' or when 'everything we learn is not exercised or done'. When highlighting such paradoxes, they described civics as 'misleading', 'not logical', 'boring', 'theoretical' and 'hypocritical' and filled with 'confusion' and 'contradiction'. Their frustrations suggest not only that their civics lessons are obsolete or even patronizing, but also that their social contract has lost validity. One argued that the laws, rules and constitution 'are useless, only ink on paper'. Therefore, 'it wouldn't make difference if I follow rules or I don't' because 'we can't relate between what we're studying and what we see every day'. Other expressions of resistance to civics were drawn from associations of politics with conflict. Some explained that they have no interest in learning about elections, laws or political systems because 'politics are twisted into personal gain'. As we have seen earlier, many showed similar forms of contempt when describing the political sphere as a source of conflict. During the class discussions, some argued that injustices in society should motivate us to learn how to address conflict through citizenship education, but the majority still maintained that civics was useless and hypocritical.

Young people also turned to the textbooks' content and curricular frameworks. They believed that many of the topics were irrelevant to their lives as active citizens. One stated: 'None of the lessons were helpful in forming our sense of belonging to Lebanon.' Others described some of the topics as age-inappropriate and present too much information 'as if we were studying law in the first year in university'. Some found that certain theme topics were repeated across the grade levels and even disciplines like sociology and, thus, found it demotivating to take 'the same thing over and over again'. Finally, students expressed difficulty in the language and terminology used. Civics, a compulsory subject, is taught only in Arabic and thus students whose Arabic is not as strong as others experience difficulties. Many stated that they 'face difficulties in memorizing things in Arabic' and understanding 'difficult vocab' and 'hard phrases'.

New approaches and ways forward

Most of the suggestions to improve their civic education classrooms asked for dialogic activities like discussions and debates. They wanted these activities to replace 'recitation', 'stop memorizing', 'not to underline and read' and have 'less memorizing' and 'less idealism'. Many argued for the omission of tests that assess how much information has been remembered and even most of the specific content in the textbooks. They also wanted it different from history class, another subject like geography that they claimed they must memorize. One explained: 'Civics must not be like history. It should be just for sharing ideas and talking about society and stuff.' The majority of their written comments further described what they meant by debates and discussions by using terms like talking, conversations, negotiating and to even 'listen to each other more often'. They believed that their conversations should be carried out in small groups and that teachers should enquire about their experiences and reflections. One suggested ways to assess debates as a replacement to exams: 'Make a debate and have our scores from the way we act in the debate and the mood that results from the debate and the way we talk in the debate.' Others suggested new topics to explore 'social problems of our society', 'politics and sexual matters' and 'things around the world not only Lebanon'. By discussing issues in class, many believed they could have opportunities to share, give advice and learn from each other. Indeed, as one cleverly stated: 'We need more discussion because civics is not a matter of book; it is a matter of life (our everyday life).' Several students viewed dialogic engagement as an opportunity to experience 'more democracy to talk what we want' and 'freedom in telling our opinions and discuss'. One argued: 'Finding the right way to use our rights in democracy, like organizing our turns to participate and say our opinion loudly and proudly without being interrupted by someone who doesn't share our opinions.'

Many urged in their responses to participate in research projects, presentations and field trips. Such activities would give them opportunities to apply and live as active citizens rather than depend almost entirely on the textbook that only presents 'theoretical lessons'. One asserted: 'We should be working practical work and throw the book away because it is a waste of power.' For activities inside the classroom, they suggested to organize 'presentations', 'play games', 'watch the news' and role play and drama 'to learn through acting some of social issues we have'. While some asked to learn more about politics by discussing what they watch on the news and establish some form of classroom governance through elected representatives 'without any manipulation', others preferred to steer away from politics and suggested either 'less politics or maybe NO POLITICS!' As activities outside the classroom, the majority listed research projects that involved 'taking the ideas of the people'. Almost all the classrooms suggested that research projects should replace civics exams. One school in the South had implemented a community service program, which students insisted they should continue. Others suggested to 'visit places that are related to our lesson' like 'courts and governmental places'.

When justifying in- and out-of-class activities, they highlighted many advantages. Some argued that 'practice activities' would let 'the students love the subject and improve their way of thinking'. Also, 'more games/activities/trips that would help connecting between civics class and daily life'. Students also wrote how participating in activities would enhance their learning experiences. Several suggested more group work and made reference to the actual exercises in the survey pack: 'Make it like group work; like what we are doing now.' Moreover, some advocated for pragmatic and collaborative learning activities because they are almost by nature spaces for living as citizens. 'Civics is about daily life, we should live and see what we're learning in order to correctly understand.' Therefore, 'we have to live it for real'; for instance: 'If we are studying about helping others, we should go and visit and help them.' As a result, these practices will 'help students in life and to let them see how things are in society' and show 'students how to deal with life and [the] problems we might face' because, as one maintained, 'we should be taught about what is really happening in our lives, not what should be happening'. Living as active citizens in the classroom by engaging in dialogues, exploring issues that affect their lives and participating in school governance are forms of critical pedagogies for active citizenship (ten Dam and Volman 2004) and opportunities to learn about rights in and through education (Verhellen 2000).

6

Teachers: Teaching Civics

Over half a decade (2006–2011) and before the outbreak of war in Syria in 2011, almost fifty civics teachers in public and private schools in Lebanon shared with me their approaches and experiences in teaching citizenship in their civics classroom. Many of these opportunities took place through semi-structured interviews, classroom observations and informal talks to reflect on what the students had done in class. The semi-structured and, even at times, unstructured conversations consistently yielded insight into three dimensions of teaching for citizenship: philosophies of citizenship and citizenship education, self-reports of challenges to learning citizenship and tensions and opportunities of critical pedagogies. Keeping in mind that these conversations took place prior to the start of the war in Syria is important. The influx of over 1.5 million refugees over a span of 4 years increased diversity to a level that the vast majority of Lebanese find as threatening to their welfare and the welfare of the nation-state. Although these teachers did not have the opportunity to experience and think about the intersection of war-related refugees and a Lebanese nationalist construct of citizenship, I reflect on this in the last two conclusion chapters based on quite recent interactions with public school civics teachers.

Philosophies of citizenship and education for citizenship

Across the country, nearly all civics teachers explained how nationalist ideologies and expressions like patriotism should ground the ideal notion of citizenship in Lebanon. The general assumption is that the national identity – Lebanese and Arab – would create a strong sense of commitment to the nation-state and, thus, Lebanese citizens would look past their religious and political loyalties

This chapter is derived, in part, from an article published in *Teaching and Teacher Education*, volume 28, 5 January 2012, available at: https://doi.org/10.1016/j.tate.2011.12.002.

that may compromise social cohesion, peace and justice. There appears to be consensus that the school is a critical space to foster principles of democracy and human rights. However, we start to identify certain tensions when they argue for collaborative and dialogic activities and advocate for the importance of memorization.

A national citizenship

Popular attributes of citizenship included 'responsibilities' and 'commitments' to the country, namely Lebanon. Indeed, they jumped to illustrate citizenship as the relationship between the individual and the nation-state even though, according to a social studies head teacher, 'the term citizenship doesn't exist in as a title in the book'. One teacher based this relationship on 'the rights that the citizen takes from his country in return for the responsibilities he has towards the country'. Others had more poetic and enthusiastic tones, such as 'to smell Lebanon and breathe Lebanon in everything'. Many also made emotional appeals to respecting national symbols like the flag and the cedar tree or when one 'sings the national anthem', 'draws something that relates to his country' or even presents an 'identity card'. Clearly, the dynamics of this relationship emphasized greater attention towards the welfare of the nation-state. 'The objective is the country', declared one teacher, while another specified to the 'protection of the country, respect of the country, improvement of the country'. The rationale behind an almost unconditional affection to the nation-state lies in an assumption that nationalist sentiments and living up to the social contract of rights and responsibilities defined by the rule of law would foster a unifying national Lebanese identity. This all-embracing, superior national identity would then help transform destructive conflicts into constructive expressions.

Nearly all civics teachers embraced the patriotic, republican concept of citizenship to address political confessionalism, which they described as a root to destructive conflict, national debility and a divided society. Thus, nationalistic sentiments would, assumingly, create a common ground that would generate a sense of unity or solidarity. In a rather concerned tone, a teacher shared her worries that '[people] are committed to a certain family or group more than being committed to their country', which has led to citizenship being a 'neglected issue' that, when talked about, is discussed 'with sort of extremism'. Some teachers described extremism in the forms of 'blind commitments' to political parties and leaders and voting for them based on their religious and political identities because they believe that the leaders will most likely work only 'for those from the same sect'. Not all found threats in the inclusion of religious and political identities as elements of an ideal construct of citizenship. Only two from the scores of teachers encouraged 'taking part in parties and organizations' and described the expression of cultural identities as a basic freedom. For another group of teachers, a nationalistic construct of citizenship would address youth emigration, a phenomenon that many in Lebanon suspect will result in a 'brain drain'. Some teachers believe that the youth are emigrating 'because they have lost faith in Lebanon'. One teacher was actually sympathetic: 'Even I, as a teacher, have lost hope in it. I wish I could travel and leave the country.'

Within a context of corruption associated with political confessionalism and other perceived minimalist notions of citizenship and concerns over youth emigration, these teachers find hope through a nationalist citizenship that generates patriotism. Most viewed citizenship as a 'cohesive agent that is supposed to tie us, as Lebanese, together', like a 'united family'. Therefore, as most explained, when the school 'encourage[s] students to love their country', young people will consider their commitment to Lebanon 'before saying that he is affiliated with a party'. Another teacher argued that by loving one's country, one becomes the ideal citizen who 'has to work for the sake of his country, not for the sake of a certain religious or political sect'. Fostering nationalistic sentiments was not the only approach to serving national interests. By 'being critical' towards political parties and their manifestos, young people can make informed decisions when electing 'the right person for the right job' and striving to 'benefit the country' and 'the public good'. This nationalist rhetoric was dominant across the country.

Only a handful of teachers talked about a type of citizenship that extended beyond the political borders of Lebanon. With 37 years of teaching experience and as a part-time teacher trainer, one believed that citizenship has a 'social implication which goes beyond the country'. Others gave more specific descriptions of a supranational dimension to citizenship by acknowledging globalization and describing it as a movement that concerns everyone, whether at national or international levels. Also within this minority group, we see a rare reference to the importance of identifying individuals as human beings 'regardless of sex, nationality and race'. These exceptional teachers appear to stand out from the dominant rhetoric of a citizenship exclusive for those holding the legal status of Lebanese citizenship. They suggested a cosmopolitan view of citizenship, but not in conflict with a nationalist one. However, teachers who defined a notion citizenship based on patriotic feelings towards Lebanon and rights and responsibilities defined by the nation-state may find a global or cosmopolitan perspective a compromise or even threat to a Lebanese national identity.

Raising children at school for citizenship

The teachers saw the school as a space that nurtures children into citizens. They described this space as a plantation, a second home and a micro-community. Citizenship education, to one, was like 'planting', but could not 'harvest' right away because learning to be citizens 'needs maturity'. Many teachers also felt that 'the school is the student's second home' and even a continuation of the upbringing and nurturing that begins at home. 'Right after the home', the school according to others is a 'small community which the student lives in'. The community was regularly likened to the 'country' or as a 'small nation' where students learn to behave as citizens from their teachers. In this mini-nation, 'students learn to implement laws and regulations' and teachers 'teach them to abide by the ethics through emphasizing their faith in equality and not in discrimination'. Most of the teachers recognized that, whether as a garden, home or small nation, the school is a critical place to raise ideal citizens or, as one teacher said, 'change or create mentalities'. The resemblance of the school to a nation echoes John Dewey's vision of reimagining and restructuring the school as a replica of the democratic system that requires children to live as citizens.

Teachers were apparently split on the role of external factors either threatening or enhancing the functions of the school. One group of teachers cautioned against the influence of home where parents' behaviours and ideas largely embrace minimalist notions of citizenship, such as nepotism. The majority of teachers expressed a less pessimistic view of the role of conflicts taking place in their daily lives. They argued that the culture of schooling should engage young people in addressing issues as part and parcel of living in a democratic society. Most recognized children should acquire the knowledge fields necessary to live with others from different backgrounds. Hence, the school should teach children moral responsibilities such as 'forgiveness' and how to 'accept and respect others' because of the 'religious and political diversification' in Lebanon. Another stressed on the importance of learning about 'other religions so we can be open and know how to talk to each other'. The majority also believed that school should have 'a great focus on environment', with very few acknowledging it as 'a global issue'.

Philosophies of teaching and learning civics

All the civics teachers expressed in one way or another a sense of pride in civic education as a subject unique in its collaborative and dialogic nature, although many argued that some information must be learned through memorization. Through critical pedagogies, civics should teach students to 'think, analyze and look at both advantages and disadvantages', especially those 'committed to certain parties or sects blindly'. Even when students 'take part in local activities organized by the Red Cross, Civil Defense Department and environmental associations', they get to see how existing institutions 'aim for the public good rather than for the interest of particular groups or parties'. Therefore, an ideal citizenship education allows young people to 'experience what they are learning' and 'live [citizenship] in the classroom and in the school'. The notion of living citizenship was also defined as 'analysing' and applying the lesson or concepts and exploring how we 'respect the laws', live 'with other people' and 'see how others think'; otherwise, the lessons 'become useless'. One of the core pedagogical approaches of living citizenship inside the classroom is through 'dialogue, not argumentation'. As almost all teachers illustrated, civics tries to 'create a sense of citizenship with the students' by letting them 'debate and discuss', 'look at others' ideas in a respectful way' and 'exchange ideas and opinions about different subjects'. More than half the teachers believed that children learn best when they have an opportunity to share what they know and then build on it based on discoveries and experiences. Similar to Freire's (1970) illustration of the dangers of banking information into children's minds, one teacher explained: 'I'm not going to tell them what is right because I'd be doing harm.' Another argued to teach 'without your personal thoughts' because 'telling them what you know and them having to take it … would then be useless'.

However, the paradox emerges when the same teachers who advocate for dialogic and collaborative pedagogies in order to live citizenship inside the classroom also argue that there *is* information that students must learn through memorization. One teacher who described civics as a 'dialogic subject' also felt that 'we can't keep getting the students used to dialogue, dialogue, dialogue' because they still have exams. Indeed, more than half the teachers explained how memorization was an integral part of learning civics. Among the topics 'they *have* to memorize' include 'human rights', 'judicial topics', 'government systems', 'some definitions' and 'laws' and, in grade 12, 'the democratic regime, media, elections, environment, immigrants and the Labour Act'. Several teachers took a rather defensive position towards memorization, saying that it does not compromise learning: 'If there is something I don't understand, I cannot memorize it' and, because 'I don't want parrot talk', they need to first understand the concepts and then 'memorize things they need to say'. Most of the teachers' beliefs on citizenship education suggest a certain tension or even contradiction between the necessity of learning to engage in discussions over sensitive issues with others from different religious and political backgrounds but within a pedagogical framework that mostly requires learners to memorize information to recite later on for assessment.

Lastly, teachers talked about what they perceived their roles as civics teachers to be. Almost all teachers described their roles in the context of class discussions and debates. One position is to allow children 'to give their personal opinion and freely express their ideas' in order to 'teach them democratic behaviour inside the class'. Another said that her role was to 'guide the discussions especially when there are people giving their opinions' to prevent 'chaos, noise and aggressive word towards each other'. The practice of guiding meant taking a neutral position. 'We have no right to impose our opinions on others'; instead, she felt her role was to 'shed light' on the topics so as to 'lighten the debate' and have it based on 'logic and civility so that it doesn't lead to conflict'. Many reported that conflicts did emerge and resulted in arguments and tension and many had to even manage behaviour. However, some teachers split on the purpose of debates. Some believed that reaching consensus or a 'conclusion' was a primary objective. Others did not believe that agreement by the end was necessary but that it was more important to listen to others 'till the end' and not 'interrupt [the other] halfway but respect their point of view'. Another role of the teacher is to 'stop the debate' if the discussions become too chaotic. Very few objected to in-class discussions on sensitive matters altogether and, thus, teachers should prevent such discussions.

Factors that challenge the learning and teaching of civics

All the civics teachers had a story to tell about difficulties they experienced when trying to teach citizenship. The issues were mostly related to the national curriculum and textbook, assessment practices and even their individual struggles, prejudices and perceptions of children's abilities. We must keep in mind three factors. The first is that none of the teachers I have conversed with so far have received formal civics training. They had specialized in subjects such as geography, philosophy, Arabic, history, law and sociology. One teacher argued it was common practice to hire 'any teacher' for the civics classroom and described it as a form of negligence towards the subject. The second factor is that nearly all teachers never took civics when they were in school, so their schemas of learning citizenship are mostly based on classroom learning experiences of other subjects. A third factor is that civic education is the only subject that is required to use the government-published civics textbooks. Moreover, very few teachers appear to supplement the textbook with other resources despite having the autonomy to do so. Their strict adherence to the book and the textbook's mandatory status by the government create it as a dogmatic source for learning citizenship. By listening to their experiences of working with the textbook and perceived limitations in teaching citizenship, we can learn more about why most teachers appear to choose to maintain a doctrinaire approach to learning citizenship.

The civics textbook

Holding a civics textbook in hand, a teacher described it as a guide to learning information and realizing 'good moral views based on national beliefs'. The teacher with 37 years' teaching experience explained that some of the positive changes in the post–civil war textbook were 'additional tools to facilitate learning', such as clearer learning objectives; more images, tables and diagrams; and more global issues such as the environment and globalization. The other teachers, however, did not share the same view, perhaps because they did not have the chance to engage much or at all with the pre-1997 curriculum. Many shared a young male teacher's view that 'civics is boring' because it lacks learning resources. The material that is available, however, is often met with discord. Difficulties that teachers mostly talked about regarding the textbook included the repetition of topics, contradictions with reality and conduciveness to passive learning. A teacher who is responsible for three consecutive year levels said with concern: 'All three teach the same thing, the same contents … [and so] students find that the book is very boring to them.' Even when the same lessons are present across the grades, 'there's no significant difference'; they are 'just a bit more expanded'. Hence, they problematize a horizontal spiral curriculum that appears to barely have any significant vertical inclination.

Teachers also reported that they and their students found topics too idealistic and, consequently, hypocritical. Students apparently resisted to learn lessons that bypass topical issues because they denounce the text in class as contradictory or hypocritical. One of the teachers recalled a time when he once pointed out a section in the book that says: 'There are no connections (*wāstas*) to help you work or pass exams.' He reported that his students immediately disagreed and protested why the book only discusses ideal situations and not real issues. Another teacher chuckled when remembering his students' reactions during a lesson on laws, democracy and rights, protesting: 'Where do you think you are, Switzerland?' In another school, students 'refused to learn civics' and complained: 'Why do we have to study civics? Look at what they're doing. They killed journalists who were freely expressing their opinions.' The same students also once stopped a discussion on democracy: '[They] stood up and said, "Miss, stop wasting your time. You get excited about this democracy issue, but, sorry, it's all a joke. Look at what's happening, there's nothing of the sort."' In summary, the book makes 'no connection between theories and practice'. The absence of controversial or real-life issues appears to generate negative associations towards the textbook. Indeed, nearly all teachers gave examples on how students expressed resistance to learning civics and how the low levels of motivation come from the paradoxes perceived between what the textbook presents and what the students see in their everyday lives. However, we can easily misinterpret the students' positions as reported by teachers. The students are not calling for a more democratic and less violent life; they merely insist on respecting them as people with dignity who have their own struggles, are aware of their surroundings, can make moral judgements and are capable of engaging (or at least learning to engage) in dialogues on difficult matters.

Some teachers found that the saturation of information in the textbooks required memorization of other top-down forms of knowledge transference that resemble Freire's (1970) metaphor of 'banking' information into children's minds. To illustrate, one teacher argued: 'There are certain things they have to memorize' such as 'government systems, what does parliament mean, how the president is elected, how we elect deputies and they elect the president' and 'certain laws'. Other teachers explained that laws had to be memorized because they are 'really, really hard' and 'very technical and difficult'. A teacher felt that the information provided in the textbook had very little room for discussion or interpretation and, thus, 'they have to memorize it' because 'I cannot change them nor interpret them the way I want'. This view of non-negotiable knowledge also applied to lessons on morals and values that are taught mostly in the form of lectures. The prevalence of banking forms of instruction could also indicate a knowledge gap in the teaching profession on how young people can build their knowledge field through critical pedagogies.

Reflections on the language of instruction reveal other critical dimensions of citizenship education policy and practice. Although few teachers associated the Arabic language of instruction with challenges of learning civics, they still revealed a sensitive discussion on the influence of nationalism on education policy. There appears to be consensus that the terminology and language in the book 'is higher than the students' levels'. From the teachers' viewpoints, students find difficulty in terminologies of the classical Arabic which differ from the informal spoken dialect. However, teachers did attribute the Arabic language to a vision of an ideal, national citizenship. Despite the difficulty of the language for many young people, Arabic *should* remain the sole language of instruction 'because if we are studying about civics in Lebanon, our [native] language comes first'. In a context of growing diversities, the post-colonial nationalist education policy of designing citizenship education only in Arabic has, to some degree, conflicted with aims of fostering social inclusion (Akar and Albrecht 2017).

Assessment issues and practices

Assessment drives learning and the civics teachers' narratives gave testimony to the weight of this claim. At the end of years 9 and 12, students sit for the Baccalaureates I and II government exams, respectively. And almost all teachers explained how these two school years are almost void of collaborative, participative and dialogic learning activities 'because we are required to finish the curriculum'. While classroom teaching for these 2 years was restricted to teaching to the test, the majority of teachers gave examples of activities and projects in years 6, 7, 8, 10 and 11. Pressures to pass government exams have even created a professional hierarchy among teachers. Schools typically allocate the most experienced teachers for 9 and 12. In hindsight, one teacher found it ironic and funny how teaching grade 12 may seem like a 'privilege', but also a 'drawback' because 'it's their last year and they do lots of troubles'.

Current assessment policies and practices related to official exams and tests taken in civics class have, reportedly, limited the importance given to civics and almost every opportunity to engage in critical pedagogies. The weight given to civics (and geography and history) in the official exams has lowered its stakes as a subject of study. As one teacher pointed out, the students are first and foremost concerned about the grades and because 'the coefficient of the grades [for civics] is not very high', neither the students nor the school administration treat it as 'major subject'. The students see civics as 'non-profitable' and thus do not feel 'interested in the subject' and 'won't give it time'. Many teachers also claimed that school administrators allow 'anyone to teach it' and sometimes allocate civics as a 'supplementary class' for other higher-stake subjects like in the maths and sciences. Consequently, students start to see it as 'an extra hour' and 'they'll ask, "Oh, sir, can we do our homework?"'. Indeed, when test scores place high value on a subject, we then believe that the subject is extremely important and, as a result, adjust the way we learn and teach accordingly (Madaus 1988).

Despite arguing that active citizenship is best fostered through dialogic and critical pedagogies, the same teachers (and others) placed great emphasis on memorization for the purpose of passing exams. One teacher illustrated this conundrum by expressing concern over failing the official exam if students only 'got used to dialogue, dialogue, dialogue', even though civics 'is a dialogic subject'. It is very rare to find a teacher who argues that students can pass the official exam without memorization. Official exams dating back to 2004 are posted online (www.schoolnet.edu.lb/exams.htm). The civics exams show four questions testing knowledge of definitions and four testing analysis and interpretation. *Access* to previous questions and answer keys, however, appears to encourage the importance of correct answers and reciting them. Moreover, some teachers suggested that learning to recall correct answers is the safest way to pass the official exams because they believe that the grading of official exam papers is often influenced by personal views or political backgrounds of the examiners. For instance: 'If a student will suggest that the government should be improved and corruption must be stopped and deputies have to resign', an examiner with a certain political disposition 'will get annoyed and annul the student's answer'. So, this particular teacher asks her students to remain 'neutral, not extremist, and to express neutral opinions'. The reported prejudices of those who mark students' official exams have threaten students to think critically and teachers to facilitate critical pedagogies.

A similar pedagogical culture is observed for tests and other forms of summative assessment that teachers design and administer inside the classroom. One teacher explained how she prepares most of the lessons and the tests based on 'memorized concepts' because she feels 'it's easier for them to answer these questions' and 'personally, I like to help students achieve high grades'. Indeed, she believes that memorizing for accurate recall during tests would benefit the children and that achieving good marks through rote learning is safer than testing their understandings. She did report, however, that not all her students support this approach and some ask for other methods of assessment. In another school, a young male teacher explained how students *need* to have teachers underline exactly what information is to be memorized. For one of his class tests, he did not identify exactly what information he wanted them to review at home and, so, 'they couldn't memorise anything ... they failed'. While he presented this story as testimony to how important students need to know the exact material they will be tested on, he also demonstrated a dire consequence of learning to learn by rote: absolute learner dependency. In stark contrast, students who exercise learner responsibility find purpose, initiative and the tools or sources they need to learn (Carnell and Lodge 2002; Watkins, Carnell, and Lodge 2007). Besides, learner dependency conflicts with the vision of pedagogy in the curriculum: 'The main aim of the new curriculum is to let the students think by themselves, but in the grades 9 and 12 they ask them about things they have memorized, this is a contradiction.' Overall, assessment has clearly shaped approaches to pedagogy to promote a surface approach to learning, which, in turn, will most likely fail to achieve the aims of civic education. Hargreaves and Fink (2006) have observed similar trends in education where extreme emphasis on high-stakes imposed targets significantly steer individuals from the fundamental intentions, meanings and purposes.

Intersubjective limitations

The teachers' stories about teaching citizenship in their classroom showed how their individual subjectivities like biases, political views, children's abilities, fears, dilemmas and conflicts with society limit many of the opportunities to engage learners in critical pedagogies. More than half the teachers shared their internal conflict of trying to remain neutral and objective when talking about sensitive issues, but sometimes found that their personal values interfered. One teacher in an all-girls Catholic school remembered the time she talked to her class about the injustices against women in India and China. 'These topics disturb me and I don't like to raise them. I feel bad for these women and I feel embarrassed to explain these issues to students.' Across several schools, teachers shared with me the difficulties of handling their own personal feelings towards the lesson on the 'Special relationship between Lebanon and Syria'. One of the teachers simply felt that 'this needs to be removed!' and another also objected to the word 'special' and told the students they could study this topic on their own because, most likely, those writing the government exams also questioned the claim. This one case of many illustrates the difficulties of teachers emotionally detaching themselves from controversial topics that are raised in class or even published in the civics textbooks.

Conceptions of students' limited abilities

Nearly all teachers praised their students' high levels of motivation and engagement, but also identified certain limitations in young people's capacities to engage in dialogic and critical pedagogies. Based on nearly all the teachers' testimonies, students generally bring to class stories of personal experiences that really challenge and enrich the discussions raised from the textbook. One teacher observed that they 'ask a lot of questions' and 'some watch the news'. Another expressed amazement at the 'unbelievable information' the year 10 students bring to class and that 'many times, they have ideas better than ours'. In another part of the country, a teacher was impressed by their 'certain openness ... towards objectivity' and how 'students are no longer close minded ... regardless of the fact that each is committed to a certain party or sect'. However, another teacher – like many – did not appreciate all the students' input, especially when their personal experiences conflicted with the ideals presented in the textbook. For example, during a discussion on citizens' responsibilities to pay utility bills and taxes, one student told her, 'We don't pay electricity bills' and another said, 'Miss, we don't pay council tax' to show that, in reality, many Lebanese evade these payments. This teacher preferred her students to give examples that only illustrated the ideals presented in the textbook; any student who does this 'becomes a contributor'. The perceived threats of real-life experiences that conflict with citizenship ideals narrated in the textbook suggest an authoritarian-like culture of pedagogy that, perhaps, even teachers are deceived by.

Low confidence in young people learning to learn

Many of the learning activities that teachers decide to bring into the classroom depend on their beliefs of students' capabilities to engage in dialogic and critical pedagogies. In one of the schools, I returned the following day for a second visit. It appeared that her students may have started thinking about the conversations I facilitated inside the class. She reported that her students asked why they were not 'allowed to talk politics, because [talking politics] is democratic'. In response, she explained 'that they're afraid of you talking politics because you do not know much about politics' and that they may fight with each other because of the views they have learned from their parents. Many other teachers share this perception of students, especially the younger ones, not having the capabilities of thinking politically or talking about political or other sensitive topics. For example, one teacher complained about her 'hyper-excited' sixth graders whom 'after 20 to 30 minutes' of explaining the lesson to them, 'they start talking, no control'. She prefers to facilitate discussions with her year 10 students (approximately 15 years old) who 'are very active as well', 'discuss a lot' and have lots to bring to the class.

Some teachers even referred to young students' limited capacities to justify learning by rote. An eighth-grade teacher believed that her students 'are still not able to express their ideas; that's why I ask them to memorize', while the 'older ones are able to express their opinions in their own language and style'. Even when the teachers acknowledge that students 'are not required to memorize' civics for the official exam, 'there are some students who don't have effective skills to understand; thus, they are required to memorize'. What stands out from these conversations is the virtual disregard to learning how to learn. The teachers did not seem to have considered teaching these students *how* to engage in discussions on sensitive issues. Their main, if not only, construct of learning citizenship in the classroom is apparently geared towards the acquisition of information knowledge that is deemed as correct or incorrect.

Institutions as barriers: School, society and home

Rarely did teachers find the structure of the school conducive to learning citizenship for diversity and living together. At a mixed school in Beirut, one teacher appreciated the mixed composition of students from 'different religious beliefs'. He believed that the diversity has created 'impressive' behaviours in the class such as how the students 'cover for each other … if someone made a mistake'. Whether or not the state of diversity generated a sense of empathy and collegiality, the behaviours of young people from different backgrounds supporting each other is, as he described, 'an ideal example of co-existence'. In a more religious-based school, a teacher found that the school's religious values reinforced principles of citizenship education such as love and virtue that also helped diffuse emotional tensions after controversial debates. On the other hand, most teachers argued that school can also undermine aims of active citizenship and referred to a government policy that prohibits discussions about politics in the classroom. Although many of the teachers openly supported this policy because it protected students from teachers 'show[ing] sides for a particular person or party', they still believed the policy should be changed. A secondary civics textbook includes lessons on political parties, civil society organizations and government systems, so 'I am *expected* to talk about politics'. I enquired into the decree that legally forbids political discussions in schools and, in response, Frayha (2008), a professor of citizenship education in Lebanon and former president of CERD, replied that 'there is no law forbidding students from political discussions'; however, the avoidance of political discussions 'is unwritten policy' so that schools avoid 'conflicts and problems' and teachers trying to 'indoctrinate students'. A prominent law firm in Lebanon also confirmed that such a decree does not exist. The illegality of political discussions inside the classrooms could well be a socially constructed myth, but it does illustrate the powerful socially constructed associations between conflicts (armed and non-armed) and political participation.

All civics teachers pointed towards their students' environment, mainly 'families' and 'the streets', to explain how external factors generate a low level of morale and motivation to learn citizenship at school. At one level, teachers found their students feeling demotivated to learn citizenship because of institutionalized social injustices like corruption. One teacher illustrated this with the common practice of people with little qualifications 'getting good job opportunities' because of 'who they know'. Consequently, students seem to lose hope that qualifications (written and experiential) and integrity will merit work opportunities and professional growth. Another teacher defined this low morale among young people as 'lost faith' and observed that students have 'lost faith in why we are studying' about the 'democratic system' and 'freedom of the media' and that Lebanon can improve. They even 'envy those who can emigrate' because, frankly, 'most of them are depressed and have no hope'. Moreover, the stark contrasts seen between injustices like corruption and exclusion in everyday life and the citizenship ideals portrayed in the book also apparently lowers students' motivation to learn citizenship in the civics class. Teachers reported that students interpret the conflicts in society as contradictions to what they are learning and the classroom discourse, frankly, stops at the recognition of this paradox.

Homes, according to some teachers, have provided children with experiences that they have shared and enriched discussions in the classroom; however, the students' environment at home was also described as problematic for teachers. 'At home, students see what their parents are doing', which teachers believe often conflict with the ideals they are learning at school and, thus, make it harder to learn how to forgive and appreciate differences. Some teachers recalled students' anecdotes that showed how daily living, indeed, conflicted with the curriculum's vision of a democratic society. Students had shared stories of how their parents managed to evade council tax and the electricity bills. Although very few teachers reported times that parents called the school, many were still worried about upsetting parents by addressing certain issues that could threaten values at home. One teacher recalled a time when parents phoned the school to complain after a class discussion on religion and asked that the teacher not spend too much time on the topic. In this case, these parents were afraid of any influence on their children's faith. Some teachers have also experienced difficulties with non-Lebanese, European families who are often perceived as liberal. However, a teacher in a Christian school located in a predominantly Muslim city in the south of Lebanon observed that the only complaints on teaching Christian values come from European parents working for international humanitarian aid agencies.

Identifying the perception of contradictions as a factor that lowers morale and, consequently, impedes learning active citizenship further suggests an authoritarian culture of citizenship education that demands students to recite information officiated by a higher authority. In other words, teachers identified the conflicts in society and at home as a problem because they make the book appear hypocritical and, therefore, we must first make changes in society and at home in order to learn the ideal notions of citizenship at school. They argued that if the government 'doesn't enforce these laws' or if parents and neighbours do not model active citizenship, then they are wasting their time teaching civics. One teacher described the contradictions between society and education as 'dangerous' because, even if you are 'stuffing the child with information', children will not have any opportunities to practice. Practice, in this sense, appears to resemble compliant behaviours rather than transformative ones. Virtually none called into question the dogmatic citizenship ideals presented in the book, let alone any efforts to question or explore these contradictions in the classroom. Any discourse on learning and teaching citizenship within this pedagogical culture of knowledge transference (as opposed to knowledge [co-]construction) would, almost inherently, overlook the absence of critical pedagogies needed to examine contradictions.

Tensions and opportunities of critical pedagogies

'Students can't wait to start this class because we can freely talk about other things', one teacher said proudly. Despite the dominant culture of pedagogy that aims to relay information on to children for the purpose of recall, many teachers shared anecdotes of lessons that took different turns. These lessons illustrated the feasibilities and boundaries of facilitating critical pedagogies inside the classroom. Their struggles also demonstrate the nature of citizenship education as a dialogic and collaborative programme of study.

Dialogic activities inside the classroom

Observing how teachers and students talk in the civics classrooms across public and private schools shows a dominant practice of rhetorical dialogues where teachers ask questions only to elicit responses they deem as correct or incorrect (Akar 2016). In conversations with teachers, however, they often overlook or may not realize the unilateral, bilateral and multilateral directions of talk during learning and teaching. Nevertheless, when prompted to reflect on what they believed were powerful learning activities, most shared stories of debates and discussions that took place in the classroom. Teachers recalled the emotions, excitement and strong commitments to political positions as positive and challenging moments. Considering the predominant practices of transferring information, it was no surprise to hear teachers explaining how the debates were 'unplanned'. Most of the debates took place during lessons on political ideologies and government systems. In one class, students challenged the identification of Lebanon as a democracy during a lesson on democratic and dictatorial regimes. The teacher observed how spontaneously students 'got very excited about this issue and directly involved their identities in the discussion'. Appreciating the discussion over political ideologies, she described her role as a 'referee' to manage the debate and make sure that her students could distinguish between the two political regimes. Her experience was more the exception.

The majority of teachers who reported on debates and discussions experienced slightly more friction inside the classroom. While many preferred to prevent in-class debates from even starting, two teachers reported on the conflicts they tried to manage and their lessons learned. In a school in North Lebanon during a lesson on political parties, students began 'throwing their ideas' and the class quickly became 'loud and chaotic'. Although she remembers feeling 'uncomfortable at the start', she became less anxious after finding she could keep the discussion 'in a civil manner' and 'not say anything that relates me to a particular side'. Another group of teachers, however, preferred to discontinue debates. One recalled an incident where students from two opposing political parties 'stood up and started to yell at each other'. She immediately stopped the fight and decided not to continue with the lesson. The students apologized and asked to continue, but 'I refused because that day the class's ambiance was tense'. In retrospect, she believes that students cannot learn to discuss and debate topics in a civil manner because they will always manage to 'politicize them'. Having almost a similar experience, another teacher remembered a class discussion on democracy where she felt disappointed to see that her students were so committed to their 'personal convictions' that they became 'aggressive and refusing to cooperate to find commonalities'. Besides feeling that she had 'failed to deliver the right message', she, like the previous teacher, now firmly believes that certain issues can be raised only with certain classes and students.

These two instances reveal a high level of students' interests and dispositions to engage in political dialogues. They also show an oversight of *learning* to engage in dialogic activities. There appeared to be an assumption that principles of respect and inclusive participation prescribed in the textbooks, for example, should have already informed young people of how to actively listen and provide evidence when making claims. Evidently, this was not the case. An exceptional number of teachers did, however, plan debates with various degrees of guiding students in how to lead, manage and carry out discussions over sensitive issues.

The few teachers that reportedly organized in-class dialogic activities had selected topics from local and international news and dedicated time for students to reflect on approaches to debating over sensitive issues. In a school in Mount Lebanon, one teacher gave her class a controversial topic to discuss and intentionally played a rather passive role as a facilitator. She described the class as chaotic with students 'shouting and screaming'. During the following lesson, she said she pointed out reasons that led to the chaos and re-constructed the same lesson but with more guidance. 'I wanted to do this so they can feel that even if there are many different points of view, they all have to listen to others, to respect others' points of view.' I asked if the students reached an agreement by the end of the second lesson. She replied saying that the students 'did not fully agree with each other' and that consensus was not the objective. 'I didn't want them to agree. I wanted to teach them about the basics of dialogue.' In another school, however, the teacher aimed at finding consensus and, thus, told the students: 'You're in charge, I want you to reach a conclusion.' This teacher explained that his interventions were mainly 'to ask someone to be quiet, to lower your voice'. In a most recent exploration into civics classrooms, I spent time observing several classrooms of an exceptional teacher in a school in South Lebanon. She designed lessons that guided her students on how to gather evidence, build arguments and listen actively when learning about child soldiers (Akar 2017b). These teachers and several others as well as some of the students during in-class conversations shared their ideas on facilitating successful debates in classroom (see Table 6.1).

Across the country, teachers who shared stories of their students engaging or attempting to engage in discussions and debates inside the class reflected also on their roles as facilitators. They all agree that topics related to politics and religion are sensitive and even controversial and, therefore, will most likely yield

Table 6.1 Teachers' approaches to facilitating successful in-class debates

Procedure	Description
Seating positions	'We sat in an intimate way to avoid clash and to allow more eye contact. When we look at each other, the debate is much friendlier.'
Written arguments	To 'write their party's principles to discuss them in class … Like a mini parliament, for three hours, students introduced their party's principles and each party criticized other parties in a democratic way'.
Ground rules	Laying down the ground rules. 'Raise your hand' and 'listening to the other' as a part of their 'freedom of speech' and with consequences: 'If I hear a single clash, I will immediately stop the debate.'
Third party	Her students wanted 'to involve a third party, a negotiator, but we disagreed on whether this negotiator should be the jury/referee or just a link between the two parties.' To have one 'who has authority … so when the debate gets heavy', this person would 'end the tensions'.

Source: Akar (2012).

conflicting narratives. The teachers, however, split in their views of how objective or neutral they should be when engaging the class in difficult dialogues. One group of teachers advocated for an objective position where teachers 'never take a side or show a personal opinion' and leave out 'personal thoughts such as telling them what you know'. By exercising neutrality, it becomes easier 'to reinforce the national identity inside students' minds'. Other teachers found that being neutral allows for more emphasis on managing the classroom 'to avoid clashes between students … and aggressive words towards each other'. Teachers also showed concern that if they do state their positions or opinions, then students may feel obliged to adopt similar views and also miss out on opportunities to construct their own arguments and perspectives. The same teachers also recognized that playing the neutral role could be 'very challenging' because it would require managing how students express and even 'defend' their personal values that are often connected to their political and religious identities.

A smaller number of teachers found value in taking a more dynamic position by playing devil's advocate during classroom discussions. One teacher had intentionally presented 'wrong ideas' to see the students' responses. Another teacher referred to them as 'brave ideas' that other teachers 'tend to hide', but students appreciated 'my frankness and honesty with them'. Very few teachers reported how their personal political views influence sometimes what they chose to teach from the textbook and how they presented it. During a lesson on Lebanon's relationships with Israel and Syria, one teacher recalled her personal objections at the start of the lesson and confirmed that the students 'didn't like [the lesson] at all', which could demonstrate the influence of teachers' personal interjections. In cases where the students expressed positions different from the teacher or textbook, many teachers felt they had to intervene in order to persuade students of 'correct ideas'. Civics teachers' ongoing struggles of trying to 'convince the students' of what is 'right and wrong' suggest a degree of controversial teaching in an education programme designed to foster citizens who can engage in critical and dialogic activities with people from different cultural backgrounds.

Opportunities of learning for active citizenship

Within the pedagogical climate of students' interpretations deemed as correct or incorrect and a curricular timetable saturated with content knowledge to be recalled for assessment, some teachers still managed to facilitate collaborative learning activities like research projects and role play. One teacher recalled supporting her students' initiative to carry out a research project. They selected topics new to their textbooks and carried out interviews to learn more about issues 'in their real lives and inside their communities'. In another school where students also reportedly asked to prepare a project on political parties, the teacher approved on the condition that the students have 5–10 minutes to present. Following the presentations, 'the discussion was amazing'. In a third school, a teacher who argued for the necessity of memorization assigned the students a research project in order to appreciate the civics class more. She expressed amazement from a report on Fidel Castro where the students 'brought some information I didn't know about'. Role play was another popular activity that teachers reflected on. One popular theme to role-play was simulating parliamentary elections by designing slogans and campaigning for the service of the school. A teacher in South Lebanon wanted to even model the guidelines of candidacy and insisted that student nominees have a clean record at school. In Beirut, a teacher reported that the students chose to address how media exploits women and, so, role-played lawyers and judges in a court case.

Other teachers designed their own activities that they found beneficial to learning citizenship. One teacher had drawn an 'option tree' on the whiteboard during a class discussion to draw out 'possibilities of where we can go' when confronted with a dilemma. Another teacher would sometimes bring in news articles and ask students to 'analyse the reasons which led to this conflict', even though it meant moving 'a little bit away from the curriculum'. Very seldom do teachers take their students out of the classroom. When covering a lesson on the justice systems, a teacher took her class to a 'criminal court'. Other opportunities to participate in activities outside the classroom included Model UN and community projects with, mostly, private universities and civil society groups like the Ecology Institute in Byblos that is concerned with 'corruption, citizenship, self-improvement, and environment'.

Paradoxes and struggles of teaching civics

Teachers' narratives of classroom learning and teaching civic education illustrate a number of tensions that help define the dominant culture of pedagogy for citizenship. In Lebanon, some teachers found it necessary for students to construct their own moral judgments and values but also expressed frustration in finding it 'impossible to convince them of what I'm trying to say', like 'what is right and what is wrong'. Almost all teachers described civics as a unique, dialogic and engaging subject requiring practice and participation; however, the majority of teachers approached civics as a 'serious subject' with concepts and ideas that students 'need to memorize'. Many teachers argued that memorization is a critical part of learning civics, although one teacher demonstrated how memorization hurt learner responsibility when the students failed their test after not receiving the routine chapter summaries to memorize. Teachers push their students to memorize information as the best means to pass exams even though questions on the official exams assess analysis and interpretation. Many teachers describe their role as impartial to allow the students to make up their own minds about controversial topics, yet the same and other teachers cannot help but express their personal views when planning and facilitating. Finally, many wanted to organize debates and even dedicated lessons to teach children how to debate; however, most teachers steer away from such dialogic activities in fear of arguments, chaos, stress and breaking a law that does not exist. Similar pedagogical tensions exist in other areas affected by armed conflict like Rwanda, Kosovo and Bosnia and Herzegovina where teachers and school administrators prevent critical discussions (or the interaction of individual knowledge) in fear of refuelling conflict (Weinstein, Freedman, and Hughson 2007).

Learning citizenship requires a pedagogy of socialization, dialogic engagement and democratic practices inside the school. However, teachers' narratives of classroom learning and teaching suggest a dominant pedagogical culture that may undermine the aims of education for active citizenship. A teacher in Lebanon demonstrated how curriculum and assessment drive surface approaches to learning. The curriculum and its textbooks present a prescriptive and, consequently, hypocritical ideal of citizenship by telling students how to feel and how to behave rather than provide opportunities in being critical or constructive. Teachers also feel restricted in facilitating dialogic activities and feel more secure with students practising to recite information for testing purposes. Based on their stories, it seems rather too simplistic to pinpoint an information-saturated curriculum and assessment-driven practices as key factors that have sustained a culture of memorization. Instead, individual and social constructs of knowledge production may have formed the ontological underpinnings of myths (e.g. law that forbids political debates in the civics classroom), illusions (e.g. official exams can be passed only by rote learning) and classroom power dynamics (e.g. teachers as knowledge-holders who are accountable for transferring knowledge to children). Indeed, the drive to measure and elicit a 'correct' discourse of citizenship in civics classrooms is significantly correlated with understandings of knowledge construction resembling Freire's (1970) notion of banking information into people's minds (Akar 2016).

Part Three

Pedagogies in Conflict

7

Undermining Active Citizenship

Students' writings and discussions about learning citizenship in their civics class and teachers' stories and reflections of teaching civics suggest how pedagogies in areas affected by conflict can indeed undermine aims of education for active citizenship. In this chapter, I argue that the dominant pedagogies of learning civic education in Lebanon do more harm than good. I develop this evaluation in three stages. First, I juxtapose the themes that emerged from students' and teachers' responses to highlight commonalities and conflicts in constructs of citizenship and pedagogical approaches to citizenship education. Second, I show a vicious cycle of efforts to transfer official civic knowledge draws young people farther away from participating in government institutions and closer to spaces that facilitate practice of active citizenship like civil society. Finally, I investigate a little deeper into the role of nationalist ideologies in Lebanon's citizenship education curriculum that aims to build feelings of unity and demonstrate sovereignty but has evidently undermined degrees of social inclusion.

Common ground among students and teachers

Students and teachers formed several shared understandings of teaching and learning citizenship inside the classroom. Probably the most common were grievances towards the national curriculum and textbooks published by CERD. Both complained about the repetition of material throughout the civics curriculum and across other programmes of study such as sociology and history. They expressed difficulties reading complex Arabic sentence structures and called for learning materials and activities that supplement the textbook 'like how in science they have labs'. Students and teachers alike frequently raised the issue of textbook that paints a perfect picture of living together but becomes problematic when it dismisses how living together looks like in real life.

Nearly all students and a majority of teachers have questioned, if not lost, their confidence in the civics textbooks. Students described the textbooks' prescriptions of an ideal democracy as 'theoretical' and, thus, 'misleading' and even 'hypocritical'. Their resistance to learning from the civics curriculum is mostly felt by their teachers. Even when one of the teachers explained the purpose of the prescriptive textbook to the class – 'Because one day maybe one of you will become a deputy or minister' – a student laughed in response: 'My dad nor uncle nor any of my relatives are ministers, so I'll never be one'. Moreover, the prescription of attitudes as civic knowledge inherently contradicts the democratic virtues of critical thinking. Students and teachers recognized this and, together, called to 'bring in the problems we face in society into the classroom' such as 'the absence of human rights' and the challenges of democracy and a 'national identity'. Examining such realities would, as the students described, make the civics class more realistic and less theoretical.

There is almost complete consensus among education stakeholders, including students, teachers, principals and ministry officials, that schooling can foster active citizenship for democracy, justice and peace. Despite the positive attitudes, citizenship education is still perceived as a low-stakes programme. At school, the civics hour is oftentimes regarded as a supplementary hour in case a maths or sciences teacher is falling a little behind and needs an extra lesson. According to most teachers, school administrators do not require special qualifications to teach civics. Students and teachers also related its low-stake status with its standing as the lowest coefficient in official exams along with history and geography; hence, they agree that civics is 'non-profitable'. Even a group of secondary school students taking the general sciences track protested that civics was 'taking time from other more important lessons to study', like math.

Teachers' and students' reflections from the civics classroom illustrated the extent to which they found necessity in managing emotions. Most favourable lessons recalled by students were those that 'touch you from the inside' like slavery, inequalities, the resistance and the welfare of the nation. Teachers, too, found certain discussions emotionally moving, such as women's roles in society. However, other emotionally related incidents demonstrated adverse learning experiences. Some students and most teachers preferred to avoid particular topics such as politics in fear of conflicts and anxiety in the classroom. More specifically, teachers lamented the emotional demands of facilitating debates and discussions in the classrooms and, thus, most prefer to avoid or prevent such dialogic activities. Teachers in other contexts affected by armed conflict like Iraq

(Vongalis-Macrow 2006), Northern Ireland (King 2009), Sri Lanka (Colenso 2005) and Cyprus (Zembylas and Kambani 2012) have also expressed similar emotional strains and struggles when confronting controversial issues in history and citizenship education classrooms.

Conflicts in classroom learning and teaching citizenship

Narrow and diverse notions of citizenship

Students and teachers showed conflicting views and even experiences when explaining their understandings of good citizenship and sharing their classroom experiences. In describing practices that demonstrate good citizenship, students mostly reported on volunteering or establishing an organization to help individuals in need and promoting sustainable living. Teachers, on the other hand, first thought of practices that demonstrate patriotism and adhere to rights and responsibilities. Students mostly reflected across multiple levels of identity while teachers maintained an idealistic notion of citizenship at a national level. Albeit the students most frequently contextualized practices of good citizenship as building for the country and making the nation proud, their responses also extended to a cultural level where participation took place through social, political and religious institutions. At regional levels, they referred to Arab neighbours and, at a wider global level, some made reference to the natural environment and even different continents like Africa. Teachers, on the other hand, appeared to mostly have the Lebanese nation-state in sight. Seldom did they make reference to cultural and global levels of feelings and practice. When the few did, they argued for a global notion of citizenship through the natural environment and advocated for a cosmopolitan dimension of having the freedom to express various cultural identities. Building on Banks' (2004a) diagram of citizenship comprising national, cultural and global identities, I illustrate the distinctions between most students' and teachers' depictions of citizenship (see Figure 7.1).

Ideologies of nationalism not only resonate in teachers' ideals of citizenship, but they have also been the architecture of education policy for citizenship in Lebanon. In 1946, Lebanese nationalism was the driving force behind the first national curriculum to demonstrate sovereignty and national belonging to Lebanon; Arab nationalist rhetoric shaped the second curricular reform in 1968–1971, glorifying the strengths of Gamal Abdel Nasser's vision of Arab solidarity and a negotiated identity of Lebanese and Arab nationalisms for social

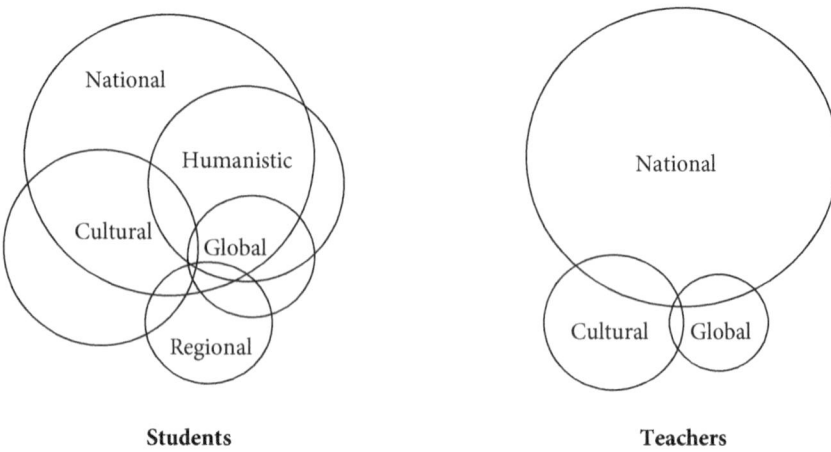

Figure 7.1 Diagram of teachers' concept of identity for citizenship in Lebanon

cohesion in the post–civil war national curriculum in 1997. Although nationalist discourses and movements can provide the momentum for post–armed conflict social reconstruction and solidarity against elitist powers, nationalism also has a dark side that can cultivate racism and fuel genocides and ethnic cleansing (Guibernau 2007). In Lebanon, the ambitions to foster a unifying national consciousness through education policy for citizenship have manifested a dark side. The Arabic-only civics, history and geography national curricula aimed to promote a Lebanese-Arab national identity either are inaccessible to students in non-Lebanese programmes or promote surface approaches to learning among students who have poor mastery of the Arabic language (Akar and Albrecht 2017).

The students' conceptualizations of citizenship that comprise cosmopolitan features and the teachers' nationalist notions of citizenship do not necessarily need to conflict with each other. Dimensions of cosmopolitanism can actually enrich rather than threaten national citizenship (Osler 2011). The advocacy of human rights and the cultivation of diversity, for example, can boost economic growth and enhance standards of living through provisions of safety, security and social justice. The pedagogical conflict emerges, however, when young people feel threatened or limited by nationalist discourse to express their various identities. A female student in a secondary school opened the class discussion with a testimony of her experiencing this conflict: 'I have an identity crisis. I was born in the States, I think I'm Armenian, but I've lived all my life in Lebanon. I relate more to Lebanon than any other country. My Arabic sucks which is obvious.

In civics, part of your identity should be your language.' Other multilingual and multicultural Lebanese students across some of the schools expressed similar concerns of the Arabic language being a denominator of a Lebanese citizenship. Their anxieties prompt a discussion on the role of nationalist ideologies in citizenship education policy, which I address towards the end of this chapter.

Knowledge transference versus co-construction of knowledge

Students' and teachers' reflections of their classroom experiences reveal conflicting approaches to knowledge construction. Evidence from the teachers suggested that pedagogies in the classroom mainly involved surface approaches to learning while students' reflections advocated for dialogic and collaborative activities as approaches in line with their conceptualizations of active citizenship. School administrators and teachers who organized community service activities, school councils and dialogues over sensitive issues were, unfortunately, the exception. The dominant pedagogy of civics classrooms is, evidently, driven by an episteme of reproducing official or predetermined knowledge to demonstrate learning. This view of knowledge *re*production is further reinforced by the pressure of accountability measures like official and class-based exams. The combination of these two factors – recalling preset knowledge and ensuring recall accuracy for assessment – generate a pedagogy of surface approaches to learning. The science behind this is over four decades old. Marton and Säljö (1976a, b) found that approaches to learning depend on *perceived objectives*, and so learning for testing encourages surface approaches (a focus on remembering information long enough for recall) while learning for application promotes deep approaches (attempts to reapply knowledge in different settings). Many teachers further championed the rote learning of information by equating the ability to engage in knowledge production, such as dialogic activities, with young people's school grade levels. The majority expressed degrees of low confidence in younger students engaging in collaborative and dialogic learning activities, claiming they 'are still not able to express their ideas; that's why I ask them to memorize'. Also, for younger students, teachers spell out exactly what information they will be tested on reciting. A teacher's testimony of students failing when he interrupts the provision of a routine summary is evidence that surface approaches to learning actually prevent the development of learner responsibility.

While virtually all teachers argued that some things in civics 'need memorizing', students described memorization as a barrier to their citizenship learning. Students presented a position on the production of citizenship knowledge that placed great emphasis on living as active citizens at school. The citizen's life, according to students, includes debates, student government at school, community service activities, field trips and, in place of exams, research projects. Students insisted on these activities because, through their limited experiences, they found opportunities to express themselves and collaborate with classmates and the teacher. Furthermore, their conceptualizations of citizenship suggest that their views of developing citizenship knowledge are drawn from their experiences of helping at home, talking about social justice issues with peers or family members and engaging in humanitarian and developmental activities organized through civil society. These dialogic, collaborative and reflexive learning activities are potentially extremely effective in developing approaches that capitalize on others' different or even conflicting ideas (Mercer 2000; Mercer and Littleton 2007; Watkins, Carnell, and Lodge 2007, cf. Alexander 2005). As expected, students argued that these activities are in almost stark contrast to memorization. Hence, based on their written and spoken reflections, they appear to find little or no place for learning active citizenship inside the civics classroom.

Dialectic versus dialogic talk dynamics

The perceived and observed dynamics of talk between teachers and students demonstrated conflicts of power and their manifestations of competing approaches to knowledge production. The evidence shows that teachers – knowingly and unknowingly – enforce a hierarchical, top-down structure of talk with the students while students maintain that a multilateral and flat dialogic approach is more appropriate for learning active citizenship. Frequently, teachers used phrases like 'convincing them' and 'right and wrong' when explaining talk exchanges between them and students. Some of the more profound reflections from teachers claimed that the students 'admitted that they were all wrong and that what I told them was right' and, from another, 'were partially convinced; at least this question will not confuse them anymore. They will not keep asking why'. Even when observing talk dynamics in the classroom, seldom do teachers' questions search for new ideas that can be built on; instead, they exercise rhetorical dialogues, which aim to seek 'right or wrong' answers (Akar 2016). Students, on the other hand, have described more willing, participative and constructive dynamics of student–teacher and student–student talk. Although some have expressed aversions to political discussions, nearly all students described classroom discussions as enjoyable learning experiences and integral functions for active citizenship. They appreciated how dialogic activities enabled them to freely express their opinions, learn about others' perspectives when addressing sensitive issues like political parties and feel they are collaborating with the teacher. Some students also argued that learning to debate was critical for living in diversity by knowing how to listen to others' stories, avoid interrupting others and talk about difficult issues. Hence, a pedagogical conflict arises when teachers' objectives of students recalling ideals of citizenship create a strictly top-down talk dynamic that denies students from openly sharing ideas and questioning others' claims.

Dialogic pedagogies allow young people to experience how different and even conflicting ideas can enrich learning and empower them as active citizens to address threats to human rights. The nature of dialogic engagement yields a conversation of sharing knowledge, enquiry and co-construction while dialectic forms of talk are designed to perform a targeted skill or synthesize ideas (Wegerif 2008). Literature on education for active citizenship also illustrates conflicting notions of talk that either foster or hinder learning to address social injustices and live with people from different backgrounds. Dewey (1944 [1916]), Freire (1970) and Alexander (2005) warned against the dynamics of talk that merely inform and seek uncritical acceptance of prescribed knowledge and pleaded for dialogic pedagogies that enable learners to actively construct knowledge together. The dialogic activities that sustain democratic living and mobilize people out of oppression are maintained by enquiry and curiosity, which all become null and void through an education of answers rather than asking questions (Freire and Faundez 1989). Dialogic practices are not just for empowering young people as active citizens; they also set foundational processes of lifelong learning, of constructing and learning to construct knowledge with others. Through the collective thought processes and social interactions of dialogues (Mercer 2000), learners find new meanings (Watkins 2005) and venture into relationship dynamics of trust, openness to new ideas and emotion management (Carnell and Lodge 2002) when explaining ideas to each other.

Civics versus citizenship education

So far, critical tensions have emerged in the students' and teachers' different and even conflicting visions and experiences of citizenship and classroom pedagogy. A synthesis of these tensions reveals another pedagogical conflict. In short, teachers mostly advocated for a content-based, nationalistic civic education that appears to contrast with the students' drives for a more participative experience that informs their maximal notions of citizenship. Their differences in conceptions of education for citizenship prompt a revision of indicators that distinguish civic education from citizenship education. By highlighting these differences, I argue that a civics educational programme, by definition, limits the opportunities for living as active citizens in school.

When civics teachers shared their understandings of an ideal citizenship and how schools can foster it, the majority depicted patriotic citizens who demonstrated their Lebanese national identity through national symbols, like saluting the flag and singing the national anthem. Moreover, they believed that feelings of belonging to Lebanon are formed when a citizen acquires the knowledge of rights, laws and obligations and, thus, 'must memorize [them]'. The teachers described provisions of education for citizenship parallel to indicators of civic education. Historically, civic education was designed to foster patriotic feelings towards the nation-state (Heater 2004). Through schooling, civics would provide students with the content knowledge of laws, rights, government institutions, responsibilities, attitudes and values necessary for participating in the national political sphere (Cogan, Morris, and Print 2002; Niemi and Junn 1998; Pratte 1988). Civics' emphasis on acquiring content knowledge compromises open spaces for young people to explore topical issues and engage in activities with peers and the community that address them. Hence, civics is often described as a minimal, narrow and even passive curriculum for active citizenship (Kerr 2000; Osler and Starkey 2005b) that yields minimal notions of citizenship depicted by passive citizens who uncritically conform to and obey laws and norms (Lawton 2000).

In contrast, the broader programme of citizenship education aims to empower young people to critically reflect on social injustices, express multiple identities and practise their freedoms as part of daily living in the school. The students' conceptualizations of citizenship and reflections of learning citizenship in Lebanon portrayed a maximal notion of citizenship addressing national, global, regional and cultural levels of identities through community service to vulnerable people and dialogues to learn about people from different backgrounds. Students also suggested a model of education for active citizenship that comprises presuppositions of universal values, content knowledge of laws, rights and historiographies and opportunities to live as active citizens through participation. These visions of education for active citizenship, unfortunately, are further impeded by the government's design of education for citizenship. In rhetoric, the Lebanese government values citizenship education as a crucial vehicle for social cohesion, and its national curriculum explicitly aims for young people to learn how to engage in dialogue, critical thinking and conflict resolution. However, the actual practices of rote learning, prescriptive textbooks and limited opportunities to engage restrict the learning of citizenship to substance; thus, demonstrating the conceptual limitation of civics as an educational subject matter for active citizenship.

A catch-22 of civic education

Students in Lebanon constructed a collaborative and participatory conception of citizenship through their concerns for individuals in need and the welfare of their surrounding communities. As suggested by Hoskins et al. (2008), this high degree of participatory attitudes may well possibly be motivated by the context of an unstable democracy. Their maximal notions of citizenship also bring to them visions and hope that could drive their participation towards social cohesion and democracy. Moreover, their visions are in line with those of the government and aims of the civic education programme that additionally want to see young people's engagement with government institutions. However, civics mostly provides dominant pedagogies of rote learning that merely value young people's abilities to recall information and prescriptive curricular materials that virtually disregard daily conflicts like corruption, violence and injustice. Therefore, the civics classroom, to a great extent, hinders or even withdraws young people from participating in government institutions, suggesting a lose-lose scenario for the civic education national curriculum. This education for citizenship catch-22 is also apparent in other countries affected by conflict like Croatia, Kosovo, Bosnia and Herzegovina, Rwanda (Weinstein, Freedman, and Hughson 2007), Cyprus (Koutselini 2008), Guatemala and Mexico (Schulz et al. 2011) where stakeholders, including parents, teachers and students of a prescriptive citizenship education curriculum expressed levels of mistrust towards politicians and political institutions.

In this vicious cycle, two actions are taking place. One is the direction of young people's degrees of participation, which are geared more towards a private public sphere, or civil society, than government-facilitated ones. Their narratives of conceptualizing a citizenship of engagement and empowerment suggest confidence and opportunities through a public private sphere comprising civil society, NGOs, home and other private institutions. This private public sphere emerges as a space for growth. Government institutions, on the other hand, have left impressions of unresolved grievances (e.g. corruption and conflict avoided in classrooms) and deceit and hypocrisy (e.g. civics textbooks presenting only ideals). This leads us to the second action: the crash between students' maximal notions of citizenship and the perceived contradictions and hypocrisies interpreted from the civics textbooks. Albeit civics in Lebanon aims at creating democratic citizens for the nation-state, students were critical of any avoidance of addressing real-life conflicts inside the civics classroom. Consequently, the prescriptive civics textbooks coupled with pedagogies for recalling preset information appeared to have generated degrees of low confidence in the government-designed civic education programme. Clearly, the civics class was not a place for students to foster a sense of democratic citizenship that enables them to improve standards of living and social justice through Lebanon's government systems. These two actions sustain a catch-22 of civic education in Lebanon. The greater efforts made to prescribe a life of sustainable peace, justice and democracy by enforcing the transference of knowledge, the more students feel deceived and withdrawn from government institutions and lured into a private public sphere that provides opportunities to engage and feel empowered.

The civic education catch-22 is further exacerbated by Lebanon's elitist government that mirrors early feudal power relations and is maintained by a system of consociational democracy and political confessionalism. Those in political power have represented confessional groups for generations, passing on family names and connections to kin who end up winning parliamentary elections. As a result, the idea of everyday citizens representing their community in parliament or other senior-level representative positions becomes fantasy land. Elitist-run democracies become a parallel world of exclusive political participation that psychologically marginalizes people by creating a sense of incompetence to gain popularity, assume responsibility and advocate for change. Alger (1980) refers to this as a myth of incompetence that elitists generate and discourages people from participating and, therefore, argues that citizenship education should empower young people with feelings of efficacy, or citizen self-confidence.

As the classroom pedagogies of civic education appear to pull students away from participating in government and political institutions, students wrote and discussed ideas that could help break the catch-22. Although some called to first resolve all the conflicts in society in order to effectively teach active citizenship, others argued for a more pragmatic approach. Many students urged for learning resources that encourage confrontation with injustices, which they believe is more effective than the magical solution of clearing society from corruption and violence a priori to learning citizenship. In practice, the everyday conflicts resulting from political confessionalism and an elitist consociational democracy would become topics that replace the prescriptive curriculum. Making transparent the challenges to addressing conflicts in government and civil society and critically and collectively exploring them in the classroom are likely to engage young people as citizens in a public sphere. Moreover, they will share a platform with government voices that facilitated these deliberations and critical pedagogies.

8

Transforming Civics and Conflict

The state of affairs in citizenship education classrooms for active citizenship in Lebanon and areas affected by armed conflict, by and large, paints a grim picture. In these contexts, governments' political agendas for democracy appear to translate into authoritarian approaches to citizenship education through dogmatic civics textbooks and the absence or avoidance of deliberations inside the classroom. Traditions of memorization and upholding content knowledge as absolute truth maintain a pedagogical culture of knowledge transference or, using Freire's (1970) figurative expression, banking information. Young people, however, living in contexts ridden with countless destructive expressions of conflict express high levels of willingness to fight for human rights and social justice. Their conceptualizations of citizenship defined by engagement to help others or improve community living could largely be motivated by the injustice they face or observe on a daily basis. Moreover, they find themselves frustrated or let down when their formal citizenship education lacks provisions of engaging in dialogues, exploring topical issues and collaborating with people from different backgrounds.

In this final chapter, I point to some directions of opportunities and approaches in reforming policies and practices that allow young people to live as active citizenship through educational experiences. I first take a look at the most established and sought-after approach to education reform: top-down changes to policy and practice. I argue that government-led reforms remain largely ineffective in transforming cultures of pedagogy from authoritarian to democratic. I then turn to high-impact teachers who give light to new directions in sustainable, educational change. The policies and practices shaped by leadership of high-impact teachers inform a grassroots theory of change that demands time and being observed through transformations in public, professional and personal discourse.

Education reforms from the top

In countries characterized by political stability, economic growth and quality education measured by above-average performance on international tests like PISA and TIMMS, top-down initiatives are facilitated by functioning and coordinated systems. In such systems, Levin and Fullan (2009) define seven key areas that determine the sustainability and effectiveness of education reform. Large-scale (e.g. government-led) education reform is sustainable and effectively helps students meet learning outcomes when change agents (1) make goals and targets public; (2) develop the strategy using a positive outlook when describing the current system; (3) engage stakeholders (i.e. government, civil society organizations, parents) to lead and work together; (4) build capacities (e.g. knowledge, competencies, resources, motivation) and the mechanisms that sustain capacity building and measure its success; (5) stay committed to priorities while recognizing the potential influence of political change; (6) openly communicate successes and challenges; and (7) use additional and existing resources (e.g. money, people) effectively (Levin and Fullan 2009). We observe these in top-down education systems around the world that demonstrate trends of improvement in raising standards and students achieving learning outcomes. A collective case study of twenty countries that have shown steady patterns of rising student achievement found that their top-down systems promote transparency of practice (e.g. teachers inviting other teachers to visit classrooms), openly report successes and failures, share performance results privately with other schools rather than public broadcast and promote a culture of collaborations among teachers from different schools (Mourshed, Chijioke, and Barber 2010).

In areas affected by armed conflict, however, government systems transitioning out of violence and into social and civic reconstruction are often too unstable or damaged to ensure mechanisms for sustainable education reform. Cultures of violence, direct and structured, that escalated and sustained conflict reverberate through peacebuilding efforts. Many of their education governance systems foster corruption to satisfy political agendas and resist devolving governing powers to local authorities (Smith 2014). Indeed, what may appear as clear corrupt practices in stable democracies are often normalized and even institutionalized as common and fair practice. In Lebanon, the selection of education policymakers in government agencies, principals and teachers is largely based on the distribution of political and religious representation, which trumps selection based on qualification (El-Amine 2004). Moreover, conflict drivers like limited professional capacities, xenophobia, sectarianism and exclusive political participation threaten and hinder curricular development for peacebuilding in thirteen countries including Democratic Republic of Congo, Pakistan, Uganda and Liberia (Dupuy 2008).

Studying education reform policies during periods of social reconstruction requires an understanding of how the education governance system works (e.g. centralized, decentralized), the school structures (e.g. segregated, integrated) and influence of donor support (Tawil and Harley 2004). Governments reforming education systems during reconstruction tend to strengthen centralized mechanisms of school governance. Efforts to govern all education systems under one authority in Sri Lanka, however, threatened underrepresentation and disproportionate support to Tamil minorities (Colenso 2005). The Kurdistan Regional Government (KRG) in Iraq has its own ministry of education that governs the curriculum and school systems in its three governorates. This self-governing authority facilitated a national curriculum that recognized the plurality of languages and cultures inside the KRG. When decentralization, however, has no larger governing authority, the education systems risk falling into a state of fragmentation as in the case of Bosnia and Herzegovina. Bosnia and Herzegovina is composed of two entities: the Federation of Bosnia and Herzegovina (FBH) and Republika Srpska where the former comprises ten cantons. Limited control by the state government over the education system has resulted in a fragmented system of fourteen ministries of education. A fragmented system of governance and localized attempts to avoid conflict 20 years after armed conflict have fifty-four ethnically segregated schools in FBH giving separate classes to Bosniak and Croats in the same school. During post–armed conflict reconstruction, international donor agencies step up efforts in peacebuilding and, to various degrees, influence education policy reform, including curriculum design. In Afghanistan, the input into the national curriculum by international experts (1) resulted in a discourse of peace that appeared foreign and prescriptive to Afghan culture and (2) fuelled the conflict as Taliban authorities resisted foreign intervention and threatened to close schools, especially girls' schools (Jones 2009).

Government representatives in the education sector in Lebanon have demonstrated how conflict drivers continue to hinder citizenship education reform. In 2010, the Lebanese Council of Ministers approved the Education Sector Development Plan 2010–2015 (ESDP), making it an official national strategy for education reform. The ESDP defined ten priorities, which were expanded from the five-point National Education Strategy (LAES 2007) that was carried out by the Lebanese Association for Educational Studies, commissioned by MEHE and funded by the World Bank. Out of ten priorities, one was 'Citizenship education' and it defined three reform activities:

1. Evaluate and develop citizenship education curriculum and learning and teaching materials
2. Develop capacities of teachers and administrators to implement an active citizenship programme
3. Develop democratic and participatory environments through parent and student councils and community service programmes

Various international agencies and governments selected one or more of the ten priorities and earmarked funds to support MEHE in implementing their reforms. The European Union allocated 1.2 million Euros to support MEHE in its reforms for the citizenship education component by providing support through capacity building to carry out the three reform activities listed above.

In 2012, the capacity-building project to support MEHE and CERD was awarded to a consortium led by the Institute of Education, London (UK), in partnership with the Association for Citizenship Teaching (UK), Centre for Lebanese Studies (Lebanon) and the Lebanese Association for Educational Studies (LAES). The consortium carried out a nation-wide consultancy with parents, teachers, students and principals; series of position papers on holistic approaches to citizenship education; and a curricular framework that was received with enthusiasm and relief by the Citizenship Committee at MEHE (CEAR 2013). However, tensions between MEHE representatives and the consortium partners revealed conflicting approaches to research, inclusion and development. One representative believed that student councils were not a priority while another resisted the formation of a Citizenship Education Steering Group comprising stakeholders from civil society, universities, NGOs and government sectors. Probably the most sensitive area of conflict was the expectation of transferring funds to the government sector or hiring civil servants to carry out some of the work, which was against the EU work contract regulations. After almost 2 years, the MEHE representative for citizenship education terminated the project of support. A few months later, a local NGO well resourced with experts in religious diversity was awarded the remaining funds to carry out the rest of the work and has managed to sustain a working partnership with the MEHE partner representatives through its own mechanisms. Although many of the reform activities have been completed, the official approvals and endorsements have been delayed.

I, like many in the education sector, believe that the EU-funded support to citizenship education reform had failed. It is not the only government-led or large-scale initiative that foundered. The history education curriculum in Lebanon, to date, remains unrevised since the 1968–1971 curricular reform. The efforts to find consensus on a grand narrative of accounts and events of the past counter the nature of history as a discipline and has, in effect, created gridlock over history education reform. Even when new policies are created, they remain vulnerable to the dominant culture of pedagogy. In 2012, a compulsory community service programme was decreed for secondary schools (Decree 8942, 21/9/2012) and required students to complete a certain number of community service hours in order to complete their secondary school graduation requirements (Decision 4/m/2013). The directive requires that students participate in a community service programme that their principal designs and MEHE approves. Clearly, the mere procedures of assigning students to carry out a prefabricated activity undermine any opportunity to empower and engage them as active citizens (Hart 1992, 2008). The new extra-curricular programme that intended to augment young people's sense of responsibility towards community development by engaging them as active citizens was produced with no evidence of teachers or principals developing approaches to implement a community service programme. Very few public schools have made attempts to facilitate this programme and, those that have, found the procedures quite vague, bureaucratic and limiting (CEAR 2013).

These failed attempts are neither exceptions nor the rule. They illustrate, however, that top-down approaches to educational change through policy or practice are vulnerable to cultures of pedagogy, institutionalized corruption and even personality and individual differences. Hence, we must invest in mechanisms other than top-down and large-scale to enhance the quality of education provisions. The testimonies below indicate directions of change from the bottom-up that are driven by high-impact teachers.

High-impact teachers as agents of change

Alongside government efforts to reform and develop citizenship education programmes, non-governmental bodies like NGOs, research centres, universities and international agencies have invested heavily in formal and non-formal citizenship education programme development. Probably the two most popular domains of change in Lebanon have been school-based reform and the development of supplementary learning and teaching resources. However, initiatives for educational change that take place in schools and provide professional development to teachers do not guarantee effective and sustainable education programme development. For example, when teachers are recruited to participate through a directive from the school principal or MEHE, the permission granted for teachers to participate becomes an extrinsic motivator and the interventions are consequently short-lived. Civic education teachers in two private and two public schools were recruited through permission letters and provided learning mentors to support them in developing approaches that foster active citizenship and social cohesion; however, many explained that their participation was mostly to support the objectives of the project rather than develop their practice (Shuayb, Akar, and Makkouk 2011). Like many other citizenship education development projects, any new approaches or materials developed have the same lifespan (if not shorter) as the funded intervention.

Experiencing and observing trials similar to the one above prompted a search for testimonies of sustainable educational change at practice and policy levels. One significant finding was that high-impact teachers have been effective catalysts of change. High-impact teachers take risks by experimenting inside their classrooms when handing over the driver's seat to students who become responsible for constructing knowledge together. These teachers go against the grain and find that students not only attain high levels of achievement but also experience the fruition of collaborating with peers and the liberations of becoming autonomous learners (Watkins, Carnell, and Lodge 2007). In the UK, the seminal 'Humanities Curriculum Project' in the 1970s saw teachers develop into curriculum makers when they participated as teacher-researchers inside the classroom and advanced disciplinary knowledge by providing learners with main enquiry questions and tools to engage in dialogues and critically challenge evidence (Stenhouse 1975). A similar discourse continues today. Counsell (2011a, b) narrates history teachers' testimonies of developing pedagogies that empower learners to produce new knowledge together in the history classroom.

Supporting teachers as change agents in developing pedagogies that engage, inform and empower young people has trickled up into policymaking circles protected by political agendas. Over the past two decades, history teacher associations in Cyprus, the Netherlands and the UK have largely transformed the curricular visions and pedagogical culture initially resisted by politicians (Akar, Hamadeh, and Makriyanni 2013) seeking to foster a collective memory at the cost of learning disciplinary knowledge (Albrecht and Akar 2016).

In citizenship education, recent studies have begun to report on high-impact teachers who have ventured into creating dialogic and deliberative classrooms that engage young people in exploring sensitive local and global issues. In a non-formal educational setting for mostly religious minority youth in Germany, Nur facilitates activities to youth groups to reflect on discrimination within a framework of human rights by expressing opinions through a human barometer, analysing how media has shaped discriminatory constructs of Muslims and Christians and exploring personal realities (Eksner and Nur Cheema 2017). Bozec (2017) presents the case of Arnaud, a public school teacher in Paris, who engaged students in dialogues and writing on extremely sensitive issues related to diversity and injustice, including different accounts of French and Algerian people during the Algerian War (1954–1962), human experiences of those who immigrated to France and the political and religious controversies in the responses that followed the Charlie Hebdo attack in 2015. In South Korea, Ms. Lim, a teacher who viewed herself as an autonomous curriculum maker, drew on *yungbokhap*, a holistic model of education that evolved over two centuries, to foster a sense of global citizenship when sharing reflective narratives of social issues we learn about or overlook through travel (Cha, Sham and Lim 2017). In Kuwait, Amani reconstructed the secondary school classroom into a space of dialogue by rearranging furniture so that students speak to each other and discouraged the practice of standing to speak; the students and Amani also found themselves 'co-constructing their curriculum' by identifying critical issues missing in the human rights school textbook (Al-Nakib 2017, 340). A case study of classroom teachers in the United States described as 'Best Practice teachers' facilitated deliberative dialogues – using evidence and active listening to discuss issues of living together in diversity – by simulating legislation where learners engage in committee meetings; follow rules of dialogic engagement; and reflect on, declare and act upon their political positions (McAvoy and Hess 2013). Concerningly, these are some of the few case studies that report on teachers demonstrating agency in transforming education and developing new approaches to fostering an active form of citizenship for living together. Below, I present one of these teachers: Nadine, a civic education teacher in South Lebanon.

Published in an edited international collection of studies examining good practices of learning and teaching for active citizenship (Banks 2017), I report on a civics teacher in a private school in Sidon who reimagined the civic education curriculum (Akar 2017b). With support from the school director, Nadine reorganized the grades 8, 10 and 11 civics lessons by taking themes from the curriculum and organizing critical pedagogies to explore the controversies and create new ways of addressing them. For one of the units that she developed, she started from the theme of human rights that appears in the civics curriculum and wanted her students to explore the struggles associated with human rights through the topic of child soldiers. Nadine chose this topic because she felt that the phenomenon of turning children into armed fighters was almost ignored in Lebanon. She wrote a main enquiry question, 'How can societies help in protecting children against exploitation?' and designed a series of lessons covering 16 class hours. The students watched video documentaries where former child soldiers in African countries shared their personal accounts and ongoing struggles in trying to integrate back into society. While sitting in her class, I confessed later that watching these testimonies were distressing. Her students, however, appeared to have habituated themselves to the dreadful stories and images. For one of the class hours, the students had been preparing for a debate on whether child soldiers should be regarded as victims or perpetrators. The 14-year-olds worked in groups to organize their arguments and draw on evidence from the films and literature. In an impressive display of organized argumentation, Nadine intervened on only four occasions to raise their hands and not diverge too far away from the argument. Towards the end of the unit plan, the students in small groups created rehabilitation centres for exploited children and drew advocacy posters to raise awareness of these centres.

Nadine pioneered a new curriculum for learning citizenship. She integrated a global dimension into a topical issue and engaged her students as cosmopolitan citizens as they reflected on their identities as children vulnerable to war and destructive authorities in power. She entirely reframed the role of time in classroom pedagogies. Rather than trying to keep up with the clock to ensure students receive as much information as found in the book, Nadine made sure that time worked *for* the students by respecting their paces in reading sources, making sense of what they are learning and creating new ideas together. She also demonstrated the potentials of developing disciplinary approaches to co-constructing citizenship knowledge; in her case, citizenship knowledge includes the methods and arguments of critically examining the controversies and injustices in protecting children as a human right.

High-impact teachers like Nadine, Nur, Arnaud, Ms. Lim, Amani and the Best Practice teachers are powerful and inspiring change agents in transforming or advancing citizenship education in areas affected by various forms of conflict. Their testimonies of students taking action inside the classroom as active citizens can inspire other teachers to question the civics curriculum, ideals of active citizenship and how classroom activities empower them as active citizens. Their trials of methods that engage young people with local and global communities and demonstrate how young people from different backgrounds can construct together arguments, advocacy campaigns and dialogues can generate a new culture of pedagogy for active citizenship. Education researchers and development stakeholders have a role in nurturing high-impact teachers by bearing witness to their personal and professional transformations (Hansen 2017) and supporting them in empowering their students as citizens engaged as co-researchers (Starkey et al. 2014). I will be bold and challenge education researchers and development stakeholders to take this role as a moral responsibility because any pedagogical revolution or renaissance that transforms the classroom into a community of young citizens begins in the classroom.

Bibliography

Abdul Samad, Ziad. 2003. *Millennium Development Goals: Lebanon Report*. Beirut: Arab NGO Network for Development.

Abouchedid, Kamal. 2008. 'Personal Communication'. Louaize, Lebanon, 3 July.

Aboulissan, Amtissal. 2011. 'Election Fever'. *NOW Lebanon*, 15 November. http://www.nowlebanon.com/NewsArchiveDetails.aspx?ID=332490.

Abs, Hermann, and Ruud Veldhuis. 2006. 'Indicators on Active Citizenship for Democracy – the Social, Cultural and Economic Domain'. In *CRELL-Network on Active Citizenship for Democracy*. Ispra, Italy: European Commission' Joint Research Center.

Adwan, Charles. 2004. 'Corruption in Reconstruction: The Cost of "National Consensus" in Post-War Lebanon'. Accessed 28 November 2012. http://depot.gdnet.org/newkb/fulltext/adwan.pdf.

Akar, Bassel. 2012. 'Teaching for Citizenship in Lebanon: Teachers Talk about the Civics Classroom'. *Teaching and Teacher Education* 28: 470–480.

Akar, Bassel. 2016. 'Dialogic Pedagogies in Educational Settings for Active Citizenship, Social Cohesion and Peacebuilding in Lebanon'. *Education, Citizenship and Social Justice* 11 (1): 44–62. doi: 10.1177/1746197915626081.

Akar, Bassel. 2017a. 'Reframing Approaches to Narrating Young People's Conceptualisations of Citizenship in Education Research'. *Compare: A Journal of Comparative and International Education*: 1–18. doi: 10.1080/03057925.2017.1396532.

Akar, Bassel. 2017b. 'Transforming the Civics Curriculum in Lebanon for Learning Active Citizenship'. In *Citizenship Education and Global Migration: Implications for Theory, Research and Teaching*, edited by James Banks, 301–325. Washington, DC: American Educational Research Association.

Akar, Bassel, and Mara Albrecht. 2017. 'Influences of Nationalisms on Citizenship Education: Revealing a "Dark Side" in Lebanon'. *Nations and Nationalism* 23 (3): 547–570. doi: 10.1111/nana.12316.

Akar, Bassel, Maha Shuayb, and Nayla Hamadeh. 2016. 'Towards a Disciplinary Approach to History Education: The Experience of the Lebanese Association for History (LAH)'. *The Peace Building in Lebanon* (13): 8–9.

Akar, Bassel, and Maria Ghosn-Chelala. 2015. 'Education for Cosmopolitan Citizenship in the Arab Region'. In *The SAGE Handbook of Research in International Education, 2e*, edited by Mary Hayden, Jack Levy and Jeff Thompson, 518–540. London: Sage.

Akar, Bassel, Nayla Hamadeh, and Chara Makriyanni. 2013. 'Promoting Educational Change in Lebanon and Cyprus: Grassroots Approaches in Policy and Curricula for

History Education'. 57th Annual Comparative and International Education Society Conference, New Orleans, LA, USA.

Al-Djazairi, Salah Eddine. 2006. *The Golden Age and Decline of Islamic Civilization*. Manchester: Bayt al-Hikma Press.

Al-Ghazālī, Abi Hāmid. 1980. *Freedom and Fulfillment: An Annotated Translation of Al-Ghazālī's al-Munqidh min al-ḍalāl and Other Relevant Works of al-Ghazālī/by Richard Joseph McCarthy*. Translated by Richard McCarthy. Vol. IV. Boston, MA: Twayne Publishers.

Al-Ghazālī, Abu Hamid Muhammad. 1980 [1097]. *The Duties of Brotherhood in Islam*. Translated by Muhtar Holland. Leicester: The Islamic Foundation.

Al-Habbal, Jinan. 2011. 'The Institutional Dynamics of Sectarianism: Education and Personal Status Laws in Post-War Lebanon'. Master of Arts, International Affairs, Lebanese American University.

Al-Jirari, Abbas. 2000. *Dialogue from the Islamic Point of View*. Translated by Jilali Saïb. Salè: ISESCO.

Al-Midani, Mohammed Amin, and Mathilde Cabanettes. 2006. 'Arab Charter on Human Rights 2004'. *Boston University International Law Journal* 24 (147): 147–164.

Al-Nakib, Rania. 2017. 'Diversity, Identity, and Agency: Kuwaiti Schools and the Potential for Transformative Education'. In *Citizenship Education and Global Migration: Implications for Theory, Research and Teaching*, edited by James A. Banks, 327–349. Washington, DC: American Educational Research Association.

Albrecht, Mara, and Bassel Akar. 2016. The Power of Remembrance: Political Parties, Memory and Learning about the Past in Lebanon. forumZFD and Center for Applied Research in Education at Notre Dame University – Louaize. Zouk Mosbeh. http://www.ndu.edu.lb/Library/Assets/Files/Catalog/Power%20of%20 Remembrance_Eng_Final.pdf

Alexander, Robin. 2005. *Towards Dialogic Teaching: Rethinking Classroom Talk*. Cambridge: Dialogos.

Alexander, Titus. 2016. *Practical Politics: Lessons in Power and Democracy*. London: Trentham Books.

Alger, Chadwick. 1980. 'Enhancing the Efficacy of Citizen Participation in World Affairs'. In *Citizenship and Education in Modern Society: Proceedings of the Symposium on Citizenship and Education in Modern Society*, 195–237. Columbus, OH: Ohio State University.

Allport, Gordon. 1954. *The Nature of Prejudice*. Cambridge, MA: Addison-Wesley.

Alwis, Malathi De. 2002. 'The Changing Role of Women in Sri Lankan Society'. *Social Research* 69 (3): 675–691.

Anderson, Benedict. 1983. *Imagined Communities: Reflections on the Origin and Spread of Nationalism*. Revised ed. London: Verso.

Aronson, Elliot, Nancy Blaney, Cookie Stephin, Jev Sikes, and Matthew Snapp. 1978. *The Jigsaw Classroom*. Edited by Elliot Aronson. Beverly Hills, CA: Sage.

Bagley, William Chandler. 1905. *The Educative Process*. New York: Macmillan.

Bakri, Nada, and Hassan Fattah. 2007. 'Beirut University Dispute Escalates into Rioting, Killing 4'. *The New York Times*, 26 January. http://www.nytimes.com/2007/01/26/world/middleeast/26lebanon.html.

Banks, James A. 1997. *Educating Citizens in a Multicultural Society*. New York: Teachers College Press.

Banks, James A., ed. 2004a. *Diversity and Citizenship Education: Global Perspectives*. San Fransisco, CA: Jossey-Bass.

Banks, James A. 2004b. 'Introduction: Democratic Citizenship Education in Multicultural Societies'. In *Diversity and Citizenship Education: Global Perspectives*, edited by James A. Banks, 3–15. San Fransisco, CA: Jossey-Bass.

Banks, James A. 2015. 'Failed Citizenship, Civic Engagement, and Education'. *Kappa Delta Pi Record* 51 (4): 151–154. doi: 10.1080/00228958.2015.1089616.

Banks, James A., ed. 2017. *Citizenship Education and Global Migration: Implications for Theory, Research, and Teaching*. Washington, DC: American Educational Research Association.

Banks, James A., Cherry McGee Banks, Carlos E. Cortés, Carole L. Hahn, Merry M. Merryfield, Kogila A. Moodley, Stephen Murphy-Shigematsu, Audrey Osler, Caryn Park, and Walter C. Parker. 2005. *Democracy and Diversity: Principles and Concepts for Educating Citizens in a Global Age*. Seattle: Center for Multicultural Education, University of Washington.

Beiner, Ronald, ed. 1995. *Theorizing Citizenship*. New York: State University of New York Press.

Benware, Carl A., and Edward L. Deci. 1984. 'Quality of Learning with an Active versus Passive Motivational Set'. *American Educational Research Journal* 21 (4): 755–765. doi: 10.2307/1162999.

Blascovich, Jim, Wendy Berry Mendes, Sarah B. Hunter, Brian Lickel, and Neneh Kowai-Bell. 2001. 'Perceiver Threat in Social Interactions with Stigmatized Others'. *Journal of Personality and Social Psychology* 80 (2): 253–267. doi: 10.1037/0022-3514.80.2.253.

Boggiano, Ann K., Cheryl Flink, Ann Shields, Aubyn Seelbach, and Marty Barrett. 1993. 'Use of Techniques Promoting Students' Self-Determination: Effects on Students' Analytic Problem-Solving Skills'. *Motivation and Emotion* 17 (4): 319–336. doi: 10.1007/BF00992323.

BouJaoude, Saouma, and Ghazi Ghaith. 2006. 'Educational Reform at a Time of Change: The Case of Lebanon'. In *Education Reform in Societies in Transition: International Perspectives*, edited by Jaya Ernest and David F. Treagust, 193–210. Netherlands: Sense Publishers.

Bozec, Géraldine. 2017. 'Citizenship and Diversity in Education in France: Public Controversies, Local Adaptations, and Commitments'. In *Citizenship Education and Global Migration: Implications for Theory, Research and Teaching*, edited by James A. Banks, 185–208. Washington, DC: American Educational Research Association.

Brand, Tamara. 2010. 'The Gendered Effects of Violence: War, Women's Health and Experience in Iraq'. Master of Arts, Near Eastern Studies, University of Arizona.

Brennan, Jason. 2011. *The Ethics of Voting*. Princeton, NJ: Princeton University Press.

Brown, Ann L. 1994. 'The Advancement of Learning'. *Educational Researcher* 23 (8): 4–12. doi: 10.2307/1176856.

Bush, Kenneth D., and Diana Saltarelli. 2000. *The Two Faces of Education in Ethnic Conflict: Towards a Peacebuilding Education for Children*. Florence: UNICEF, Innocenti Research Centre.

Campanini, Massimo. 1996. 'Al-Ghazzālī'. In *History of Islamic Philosophy*, edited by Seyyed Hossein Nasr and Oliver Leaman, 258–274. London: Routledge.

Caritas Lebanon Migrant Center. 2014. 'Left Behind: Iraqi Refugees in Lebanon'. https://www.caritas.org/2014/10/left-behind-iraqi-refugees-lebanon/.

Carnell, Eileen, and Caroline Lodge. 2002. *Supporting Effective Learning*. London: Paul Chapman Publishing.

CEAR. 2013. Support to the Lebanese Education Reform: Citizenship Education (EuropeAid/131916/M/ACT/LB). Beirut, Lebanon: Unpublished.

Cerasoli, Christopher P., Jessica M. Nicklin, and Michael T. Ford. 2014. 'Intrinsic Motivation and Extrinsic Incentives Jointly Predict Performance: A 40-year Meta-Analysis'. *Psychological bulletin* 140 (4): 980–1008. doi: 10.1037/a0035661.

Cha, Yun-Kyung, Seung-Hwan Sham, and Mi-Eun Lim. 2017. 'Citizenship Education in Korea: Challenges and New Possibilities'. In *Citizenship Education and Global Migration: Implications for Theory, Research and Teaching*, edited by James A. Banks, 237–253. Washington, DC: American Educational Research Association.

Chapman, Arthur. 2002. 'Camels, Diamonds and Counterfactuals: A Model for Teaching Causal Reasoning'. *Teaching History* 112: 46–53.

Chase, Anthony., and Amr Hamzawy, eds. 2006. *Human Rights in the Arab World: Independent Voices*. Philadelphia: University of Pennsylvania Press.

Chase, Anthony, and Kyle Ballard. 2006. 'Appendix 2: Status of Human Rights Treaty Ratifications, with Notable Reservations, Understandings and Declarations'. In *Human Rights in the Arab World: Independent Voices*, edited by Anthony Chase and Amr Hamzawy, 237–282. Philadelphia: University of Pennsylvania Press.

Churchill, Stacy. 1986. *The Education of Linguistic and Cultural Minorities in the OECD Countries*. Clevedon: Multilingual Matters.

Coffield, Frank J., David Moseley, Elaine Hall, and Kathryn Ecclestone. 2004a. *Learning Styles and Pedagogy in Post-16 Learning: A Systematic and Critical Review*. London: Learning and Skills Research Centre/University of Newcastle upon Tyne.

Coffield, Frank, David Moseley, Elaine Hall, and Kathryn Ecclestone. 2004b. *Should We Be Using Learning Styles? What Research Has to Say to Practice*. London: Learning and Skills Research Centre.

Cogan, John, Paul Morris, and Murray Print. 2002. 'Civic Education in the Asia-Pacific Region: An Introduction'. In *Civic Education in the Asia-Pacific Region: Case Studies Across Six Societies*, edited by John Cogan, Paul Morris and Murray Print, 1–22. New York: RoutledegeFalmer.

Colenso, Peter. 2005. 'Education and Social Cohesion: Developing a Framework for Education Sector Reform in Sri Lanka'. *Compare: A Journal of Comparative and International Education* 35 (4): 411–428.

Counsell, Christine. 2011a. 'Disciplinary Knowledge for All, the Secondary History Curriculum and History Teachers' Achievement'. *The Curriculum Journal* 22 (2): 201–225.

Counsell, Christine. 2011b. 'History Teachers as Curriculum Makers: Professional Problem-Solving in Secondary School History Education in England'. In *Patterns of Research in Civics, History, Geography and Religious Education*, edited by Bengt Schüllerqvist, 53–88. Karlstad: Karlstad University Press.

Crick, Bernard. 2000. *Essays on Citizenship*. London: Continuum.

Curle, Adam. 1971. *Making Peace*. London: Tavistock Publications.

Dannreuther, Ronald. 1999. 'Cosmopolitan Citizenship and the Middle East'. In *Cosmopolitan Citizenship*, edited by Andrew Linklater, 143–167. London: Macmillan Press.

DeCuir-Gunby, Jessica, and Meca Williams. 2007. 'The Impact of Race and Racism on Students' Emotions: A Critical Race Analysis'. In *Emotion in Education*, edited by Paul Schutz and Reinhard Pekrun, 205–219. Burlington, MA: Academic Press.

Delors, Jacques. 1996. 'Education: The Necessary Utopia'. In *Learning: The Treasure Within: Report to UNESCO of the International Commission on Education for the Twenty-first Century*, edited by Jacques Delors, In'am Al Mufti, Isao Amagi, Roberto Carneiro, Fay Chung, Bronislaw Geremek, William Gorham, Aleksandra Kornhauser, Michael Manley, Marisela Padrón Quero, Marie-Angélique Savané, Karan Singh, Rodolfo Stavenhagen, Myong Won Suhr and Zhou Nanzhao, 13–35. Paris: UNESCO Publishing.

Delors, Jacques, In'am Al Mufti, Isao Amagi, Roberto Carneiro, Fay Chung, Bronislaw Geremek, William Gorham, Aleksandra Kornhauser, Michael Manley, Marisela Padrón Quero, Marie-Angélique Savané, Karan Singh, Rodolfo Stavenhagen, Myong Won Suhr, and Zhou Nanzhao, eds. 1996. *Learning: The Treasure Within: Report to UNESCO of the International Commission on Education for the Twenty-first Century*. Paris: UNESCO Publishing.

Dennison, Bill, and Roger Kirk. 1990. *Do, Review, Learn, Apply: A Simple Guide to Experiential Learning*. Oxford: Blackwell.

Dewey, John. 1897. *My Pedagogic Creed*. New York: E. L. Kellogg.

Dewey, John. 1938. *Experience and Education*. New York: Macmillan.

Dewey, John. 1944 [1916]. *Democracy and Education: An Introduction to the Philosophy of Education*. 28th printing, reprinted 1955 ed, *Text-book series*. New York: Macmillan.

Donne, John. 1987 [1624]. *Devotions upon Emergent Occasions*. Edited by A. Raspa. Oxford: Oxford University Press.

Dudouet, Veronique. 2006. 'Title'. Berghof Report Nr. 15, Berlin.

Dupuy, Kendra. 2008. *Education for Peace: Building Peace and Transforming Armed Conflict through Education Systems*. Oslo: Save the Children and PRIO.

Edwards, John. 2009. *Language and Identity: Key Topics in Sociolinguistics*. Cambridge: Cambridge University Press.

Eksner, H. Julia, and Saba Nur Cheema. 2017. '"Who Here Is a Real German?" German Muslim Youths, Othering, and Education'. In *Citizenship Education and Global Migration: Implications for Theory, Research and Teaching*, edited by James A. Banks, 161–183. Washington, DC: American Educational Research Association.

El-Amine, Adnan. 2004. 'Educational Reform: Nine Principles and Five Issues'. In *Options for Lebanon*, edited by Nawwāf Salam, 209–254. London: Centre for Lebanese Studies and I. B. Tauris.

El-Jisr, Karim, and Capricia Chabarekh. 2012. 'Title'. Sustainable Development in Lebanon: Status and Vision, Republic of Lebanon.

European Commission. 2018. 'Proposal for a Council Recommendation on Key Competences for Lifelong Learning'. Brussels: European Commission. https://ec.europa.eu/education/sites/education/files/recommendation-key-competences-lifelong-learning.pdf.

European Parliament and Council. 2006. 'Recommendation of the European Parliament and of the Council of 18 December 2006 on Key Competences for Lifelong Learning (2006/962/EC)'. *Official Journal of the European Union* 49: 10.

Faour, Muhammad, and Marwan Muasher. 2011. 'Education for Citizenship in the Arab World: Key to the Future'. In *The Carnegie Papers*. Beirut: Carnegie Middle East Center.

Firro, Kais M. 2004. 'Lebanese Nationalism versus Arabism: From Bulus Nujaym to Michel Chiha'. *Middle Eastern Studies* 40 (5): 1–27.

Fontana, Giuditta. 2017. *Education Policy and Power-Sharing in Post-Conflict Societies*. DE: Springer Nature.

Francis, Diane. 2002. *People, Peace and Power: Conflict Transformation in Action*. London: Pluto Press.

Frayha, Nemer. 1985. 'Religious Conflict and the Role of Social Studies for Citizenship Education in the Lebanese Schools between 1920 and 1983'. PhD thesis, School of Education, Stanford University.

Frayha, Nemer. 2003. 'Education and Social Cohesion in Lebanon'. *Prospects* 33 (1): 77–88.

Frayha, Nemer. 2004. 'Developing Curriculum as a Means to Bridging National Divisions in Lebanon'. In *Education, Conflict and Social Cohesion*, edited by Sobhi Tawil and Alexandra Harley, 159–205. Geneva: UNESCO International Bureau of Education.

Frayha, Nemer. 2008. 'Personal Communication'. 5 May, 2008.

Freire, Paulo. 1970. *Pedagogy of the Oppressed*. London: The Continuum Publishing Company.

Freire, Paulo, and Antonio Faundez. 1989. *Learning to Question*. New York: The Continuum Publishing Company.

Frisch, Hillel. 2001. 'Middle East'. In *Encyclopedia of Nationalism: Fundamental Themes*, edited by Alexander J. Motyl. San Diego, CA: Academic Press.

Galtung, Johan. 1969. 'Violence, Peace, and Peace Research'. *Journal of Peace Research* 6 (3): 167–191.

Galtung, Johan. 1990. 'Cultural Violence'. *Journal of Peace Research* 27 (3): 291–305.

Galtung, Johan. 1996. *Peace by Peaceful Means: Peace and Conflict, Development and Civilization*. London: Sage.

Gambill, Gary. 2003. 'Student Politics in Lebanon'. *Middle East Intelligence Bulletin*, 3 November. Accessed 23 February 2012. http://www.meforum.org/meib/articles/0311_l1.htm.

Gest, Justin, and Sean W. D. Gray. 2015. 'Silent Citizenship: The Politics of Marginality in Unequal Democracies'. *Citizenship Studies* 19 (5): 465–473. doi: 10.1080/13621025.2015.1074344.

Ghalyoun, Burhan. 2009. 'Human Rights in Contemporary Arabic Thought'. In *Human Rights in Arab Thought: A Reader*, edited by Salma Khadra Jayyusi, 343–373. London: I. B. Tauris.

Gillies, Robyn M. 2017. 'Promoting Academically Productive Student Dialogue during Collaborative Learning'. *International Journal of Educational Research*. doi: https://doi.org/10.1016/j.ijer.2017.07.014.

Giroux, Henry. 2001. *Theory and Resistance in Education: Towards a Pedagogy for the Opposition*. Revised and expanded ed. Westport, CT: Bergin & Garvey.

Glendon, Mary Anne. 2000. 'Introduction'. In *The Challenge of Human Rights: Charles Malik and the Universal Declaration*, edited by Charles Habib Malik, 1–9. Oxford: Charles Malik Foundation; Centre for Lebanese Studies.

Goodman, James. 2007. 'Reflexive Solidarities: Between Nationalism and Globalism'. In *Nationalism and Global Solidarities: Alternative Projections to Neoliberal Globalisation*, edited by James Goodman and Paul James, 187–204. Oxon: Routledge.

Gross, Zehavit, and Lynn Davies, eds. 2015. *The Contested Role of Education in Conflict and Fragility*. Rotterdam: Sense Publishers.

Guibernau, Montserrat. 2007. *The Identity of Nations*. Cambridge: Polity Press.

Gutmann, Amy. 2004. 'Unity and Diversity in Democratic Multicultural Education'. In *Diversity and Citizenship Education: Global Perspectives*, edited by James Banks, 71–96. San Francisco, CA: Jossey-Bass.

Habermas, Jürgen. 1984 [1981]. *The Theory of Communicative Action, Volume 1: Reason and Rationalization of Society*. Translated by Thomas McCarthy. Boston, MA: Beacon Press.

Habermas, Jürgen. 1995. 'Citizenship and National Identity: Some Reflections on the Future of Europe'. In *Theorizing Citizenship*, edited by Ronald Beiner, 255–281. Albany, NY: State University of New York Press.

Hahn, Carole. 2010. 'Comparative Civic Education Research: What We Know and What We Need to Know'. *Citizenship Teaching and Learning* 6 (1): 5–23.

Halbwachs, Maurice. 1950. *La mémoire Collective*. Paris: Presses Universitaires de France.

Hamad, Al-Nour. 2009. 'The Islamic Intellectual Mahmoud Muhammad Taha on the Impasse of Human Rights in Islamic Legislation'. In *Human Rights in Arab Thought: A Reader*, edited by Salma Khadra Jayyusi, 324–339. London: I. B. Tauris.

Hankiss, Elemer. 2004. '*Paideia* in an Age of Uncertainty'. In *Educating for Democracy: Paideia in an Age of Uncertainty*, edited by Alan M. Olson, David M. Steiner and Irina S. Tuuli, 149–162. Lanham, MD: Rowman Littlefield Publishers.

Hansen, David T. 2017. 'Bearing Witness to Teaching and Teachers'. *Journal of Curriculum Studies* 49 (1): 7–23. doi: 10.1080/00220272.2016.1205137.

Haque, Amber. 2004. 'Psychology from Islamic Perspective: Contributions of Early Muslim Scholars and Challenges to Contemporary Muslim Psychologists'. *Journal of Religion and Health* 43 (4): 357–377.

Harber, Clive. 2004. *Schooling as violence: How Schools Harm Pupils and Societies*. Oxon: RoutledgeFalmer.

Härdig, Anders. 2011. 'The Evolutionaries: Transforming the Political System and Culture in Lebanon'. Doctor of Philosophy in International Relations, Faculty of the School of International Service, American University.

Hargreaves, Andrew, and Dean Fink. 2006. *Sustainable Leadership*. San Francisco, CA: Jossey-Bass.

Hart, Roger. 1992. 'Children's Participation: From Tokenism to Citizenship'. In *Innocenti Essays, No. 4*. Florence: UNICEF, International Child Development Centre.

Hart, Roger. 2008. 'Stepping Back from "the ladder": Reflections on a Model of Participatory Work with Children'. In *Participation and Learning*, edited by Alan A. Reid, Bjarne Bruun Jensen, Jutta Nikel and Venka Simovska, 19–31. Dordrecht, The Netherlands: Springer.

Hayward, Jeremy. 2009. 'Beginning to Teach Citizenship'. In *Learning to Teach Citizenship in the Secondary School: A Companion to School Experience*, edited by Liam Gearon, 53–63. London: Taylor & Francis.

Heater, Derek. 2004. *Citizenship: The Civic Ideal in World History, Politics and Education*. Third ed. Manchester: Manchester University Press.

Hirsch, Eric Donald. 1988. *Cultural Literacy: What Every American Needs to Know*. New York: Random House.

Hitti, Philip. 1967. *Lebanon in History: From the Earliest Times to the Present*. Third ed. New York: St Martin's Press.

Hoskins, Bryony. 2006. Active Citizenship for Democracy: Report of the Second Research Network Meeting. Strasbourg: Council of Europe.

Hoskins, Bryony. 2013. 'What Does Democracy Need from Its Citizens?' In *Civic Education and Competences for Engaging Citizens in Democracies*, edited by Murray Print and Dirk Lange, 23–35. Rotterdam: Sense Publishers.

Hoskins, Bryony, Ernesto Villalba, Daniel Van Nijlen, and Carolyn Barber. 2008. *Measuring Civic Competence in Europe: A Composite Indicator Based on IEA Civic Education Study 1999 for 14 Years Old in School*. Luxembourg: European Communities.

Hoskins, Bryony, Hermann Abs, Christine Han, David Kerr, and Wiel Veugelers. 2012. Contextual Report: Participatory Citizenship in the European Union, Institute of Education report for EU. Southampton: Southampton University.

Hoskins, Bryony, and Ruth Deakin Crick. 2010. 'Competences for Learning to Learn and Active Citizenship: Different Currencies or Two Sides of the Same Coin?' *European Journal of Education* 45 (1): 121–137.

Hourani, Albert. 1991. *A History of the Arab Peoples*. London: Faber & Faber.

Hourani, Guita, Liliane Haddad, and Elias Sfeir. 2011. 'Title'. Workshop on Lebanese Migration in the World, Zouk Mikhayel.

Ibn Khaldūn. 2005 [1370]. *The Muqaddimah: An Introduction to History*. Translated by Franz Rosenthal. Princeton, NJ: Princeton University Press.

Inter-Parliamentary Union. 2018. Women in National Parliaments. Geneva: Inter-Parliamentary Union.

Isin, Engin, and Bryan Turner. 2002. 'Citizenship Studies: An Introduction'. In *Handbook of Citizenship Studies*, edited by Engin Isin and Bryan Turner, 1–10. London: Sage.

Isin, Engin, and Bryan Turner. 2007. 'Investigating Citizenship: An Agenda for Citizenship Studies'. *Citizenship Studies* 11 (1): 5–17. doi: 10.1080/13621020601099773.

Jabbour, Khayrazad Kari. 2014. 'Civic Education in Lebanon'. *Bulgarian Journal of Science and Education Policy* 8 (2): 392–407.

Janmyr, Maja. 2017. 'No Country of Asylum: 'Legitimizing' Lebanon's Rejection of the 1951 Refugee Convention'. *International Journal of Refugee Law* 29 (3): 438–465. doi: 10.1093/ijrl/eex026.

Janoski, Thomas, and Brian Gran. 2002. 'Political Citizenship: Foundations of Rights'. In *Handbook of Citizenship Studies*, edited by Engin Isin and Bryan Turner, 13–52. London: Sage.

Jones, Adele. 2009. 'Curriculum and Civil Society in Afghanistan'. *Harvard Educational Review* 79 (1): 113–168.

Joseph, Suad. 1999a. 'Descent of the Nation: Kinship and Citizenship in Lebanon'. *Citizenship Studies* 3 (3): 295–318.

Joseph, Suad. 1999b. 'Gender and Citizenship in Muslim Communities: Introduction'. *Citizenship Studies* 3 (3): 293–294.

Joseph, Suad. 1999c. 'Gendering Citizenship in the Middle East'. In *Gender and Citizenship in the Middle East*, edited by Suad Joseph, 3–30. New York: Syracuse University Press.

Joseph, Suad. 2005. 'Teaching Rights and Responsibilities: Paradoxes of Globalization and Children's Citizenship in Lebanon'. *Journal of Social History* 38 (4): 1007–1026.

Kamis, Mazalan, and Mazanah Muhammad. 2007. 'Islam's Lifelong Learning Mandate'. In *Non-Western Perspectives on Learning and Knowing*, edited by Sharan B. Merriam, 21–40. Malabar, FL: Krieger.

Kant, Immanuel. 2006 [1795]. *Toward Perpetual Peace: A Philosophical Sketch*. New Haven, CT: Yale University Press.

Kaufman, Asher. 2001. 'Pheonicianism: The Formation of an Identity in Lebanon of 1920'. *Middle Eastern Studies* 37 (1): 173–194. doi: 10.1080/714004369.

Kennedy, Kerry J. 2007. 'Student Constructions of "Active Citizenship": What Does Participation Mean to Students?' *British Journal of Educational Studies* 55 (3): 304–324.

Kerr, David. 2000. 'Citizenship Education: An International Comparison'. In *Education for Citizenship*, edited by Denis Lawton, Jo Cairns and Roy Gardner, 200–227. London: Continuum.

Khalidi, Tarif. 1985. *Classical Arab Islam: The Culture and Heritage of the Golden Age.* Princeton, NJ: Darwin Press.

Khalidi, Tarif. 1992. 'Religion and Citizenship in Islam'. In *Religion and Citizenship in Europe and the Arab World*, edited by Jørgen S. Nielsen, 25–30. London: Grey Seal.

Khātami, Mohammad. 2000. *Islam, Dialogue and Civil Society.* Canberra: Australian National University.

King, John T. 2009. 'Teaching and Learning about Controversial Issues: Lessons from Northern Ireland'. *Theory & Research in Social Education* 37 (2): 215–246. doi: 10.1080/00933104.2009.10473395.

Kirby, Perpetua, Claire Lanyon, Kathleen Cronin, and Ruth Sinclair. 2003. Building a Culture of Participation: Involving Children and Young People in Policy, Service Planning, Delivery and Evaluation. London: Department for Education and Skills.

Kivisto, Peter, and Thomas Faist. 2007. *Citizenship: Discourse, Theory, and Transnational Prospects.* Malden, MA: Blackwell Publishing.

Kiwan, Dina. 2008. 'Citizenship Education in England at the Cross-Roads? Four Models of Citizenship and Their Implications for Ethnic and Religious Diversity'. *Oxford Review of Education* 34 (1): 39–58.

Kleingeld, Pauline. 2006. 'Editor's Introduction: Kant on Politics, Peace, and History'. In *Toward Perpetual Peace and Other Writings on Politics, Peace, and History*, edited by Pauline Kleingeld, xv–xxiv. New Haven, CT: Yale University Press.

Koutselini, Mary. 2008. 'Citizenship Education in Context: Student Teacher Perceptions of Citizenship in Cyprus'. *Intercultural Education* 19 (2): 163–175. doi: 10.1080/14675980801889690.

Kymlicka, Will. 1996. *Multicultural Citizenship: A Liberal Theory of Minority Rights.* Oxford: Oxford University Press.

Kymlicka, Will. 2001. *Politics in the Vernacular: Nationalism, Multiculturalism and Citizenship.* Oxford: Oxford University Press.

LAES. 2003. *Evaluation of the New Curriculum in Lebanon.* Vol. 2. Beirut: LAES.

LAES. 2006. *National Education Strategy in Lebanon: Vision Document.* Beirut: Lebanese Association for Education Studies.

LAES. 2007. *National Education Strategy in Lebanon: Vision Document.* Beirut: Lebanese Association for Educational Studies.

Lawton, Denis. 2000. 'Overview: Citizenship Education in Context'. In *Education for Citizenship*, edited by Denis Lawton, Jo Cairns and Roy Gardner, 9–13. London: Continuum.

Lebanese Constitution. 1997. 'The Lebanese Constitution'. *Arab Law Quarterly* 12 (2): 224–261.

Lebanon Crisis Response Plan. 2015. 'Situation Overview'. *Monthly Dashboard,* July. Accessed 13 October 2015. http://data.unhcr.org/syrianrefugees/download. php?id=9505.

Lederach, John Paul. 2005. *The Moral Imagination: The Art and Soul of Building Peace.* Oxford: Oxford University Press.

Leman, Patrick J., and Gerard Duveen. 1999. 'Representations of Authority and Children's Moral Reasoning'. *European Journal of Social Psychology* 29 (5–6): 557–575. doi:10.1002/(SICI)1099-0992(199908/09)29:5/6<557::AID-EJSP946>3.0.CO;2-T.

Levin, Ben, and Michael Fullan. 2009. 'Learning About System Renewal'. In *The Challenge of Change: Start School Improvement Now!,* edited by Michael Fullan. Thousand Oaks, CA: Corwin Press.

Linklater, Andrew. 2002. 'Cosmopolitan Citizenship'. In *Handbook of Citizenship Studies,* edited by Engin Isin and Bryan Turner, 317–332. London: Sage.

Lombard, Maurice. 1975. *The Golden Age of Islam.* Translated by Joan Spencer. Amsterdam: North-Holland Publishing.

Lund, Michael. 1996. *Preventing Violent Conflicts: A Strategy for Preventive Democracy.* Washington, DC: United States Institute of Peace Press.

Madaus, George. 1988. 'The Influence of Testing on the Curriculum'. In *Critical Issues in Curriculum,* edited by Laurel N. Tanner, 83–117. Chicago: University of Chicago Press.

Marshall, Thomas H. 1950. *Citizenship and Social Class and Other Essays.* Cambridge: University Press.

Marton, Ference, and Roger Säljö. 1976a. 'On Qualitative Differences in Learning. I: Outcome and Process'. *British Journal of Educational Psychology* 46: 4–11.

Marton, Ference, and Roger Säljö. 1976b. 'On Qualitative Differences in Learning. II: Outcome as a Function of the Learner's Conception of the Task'. *British Journal of Educational Psychology* 46: 115–127.

Massialas, Byron, and Samir Jarrar. 1983. *Education in the Arab World.* New York: Praeger Publishers.

Mattar, Mohammed. 2007. 'Is Lebanese Confessionalism to Blame?' In *Breaking the Cycle: Civil Wars in Lebanon,* edited by Youssef Choueiri, 47–66. London: Stacey International.

McAvoy, Paula, and Diana Hess. 2013. 'Classroom Deliberation in an Era of Political Polarization'. *Curriculum Inquiry* 43 (1): 14–47. doi: 10.1111/curi.12000.

McCowan, Tristan. 2012. 'Human Rights within Education: Assessing the Justifications'. *Cambridge Journal of Education* 42 (1): 67–81. doi: 10.1080/0305764X.2011.651204.

McLaughlin, Terence. 1992. 'Citizenship, Diversity and Education: A Philosophical Perspective'. *The Journal of Moral Education, Special Issue: Citizenship and Diversity* 21 (3): 235–250.

Meer, Shamin, and Charlie Sever. 2004. *Gender and Citizenship: Overview Report.* Institute of Development Studies. London. http://www.bridge.ids.ac.uk/sites/bridge. ids.ac.uk/files/reports/Citizenship-report.pdf

Mercer, Neil. 1995. *The Guided Construction of Knowledge.* Clevedon: Multilingual Matters.

Mercer, Neil. 2000. *Words and Minds: How We Use Language to Think Together.* London: Routledge.

Mercer, Neil, and Karen Littleton. 2007. *Dialogue and the Development of Children's Thinking: A Sociocultural Approach.* London: Routledge.

Miller, David. 2000. *Citizenship and National Identity.* Cambridge: Polity Press.

Ministry of Education and Higher Education [Lebanon]. 1997. *Curricula of General Education and Their Aims.* Beirut: Center for Educational Research and Development.

Mohammed, Naqi. 2005. *Modern Philosophy of Education.* New Delhi: Anmol Publications.

Moore, Alex. 2013. 'Love and Fear in the Classroom: How "Validating Affect" Might Help Us Understand Young Students and Improve Their Experiences of School Life and Learning'. In *The Uses of Psychoanalysis in Working with Children's Emotional Lives*, edited by Michael O'Loughlin, 285–304. Plymouth: Rowman and Littlefield.

Mourshed, Mona, Chinezi Chijioke, and Michael Barber. 2010. 'How the World's Most Improved School Systems Keep Getting Better'. McKinsey. https://www.mckinsey. com/industries/social-sector/our-insights/how-the-worlds-most-improved-school-systems-keep-getting-better.

Mukamana, Donatilla, and Petra Brysiewicz. 2008. 'The Lived Experience of Genocide Rape Survivors in Rwanda'. *Journal of Nursing Scholarship* 40 (4): 379–384. doi: 10.1111/j.1547-5069.2008.00253.x.

Näykki, Piia, Sanna Järvelä, Paul A. Kirschner, and Hanna Järvenoja. 2014. 'Socio-emotional Conflict in Collaborative Learning—A Process-Oriented Case Study in a Higher Education Context'. *International Journal of Educational Research* 68 (Supplement C): 1–14. doi: https://doi.org/10.1016/j.ijer.2014.07.001.

Niemi, Richard, and Jane Junn. 1998. *Civic Education: What Makes Students Learn.* New Haven, CT: Yale University Press.

Niemiec, Christopher P., and Richard M. Ryan. 2009. 'Autonomy, Competence, and Relatedness in the Classroom: Applying Self-Determination Theory to Educational Practice'. *School Field* 7 (2): 133–144. doi: 10.1177/1477878509104318.

Nixon, Michael, Hannah Peterson, Daniel Woods, Dina Reventlow, and Theis Lykkegaard. 2007. 'Confessionalism: An Inherently Flawed Ideal or an Answer to Ethnically Diverse Countries?' Accessed 10 July. http://diggy.ruc.dk/ bitstream/1800/3168/1/Confessionalism.pdf.

Novelli, Mario, Mieke T. A. Lopes Cardozo, and Alan Smith. 2015. 'A Theoretical Framework for Analysing the Contribution of Education to Sustainable Peacebuilding: 4Rs in Conflict-Affected Contexts'. University of Amsterdam. http:// learningforpeace.unicef.org/partners/research-consortium/research-outputs/.

Nussbaum, Martha. 1997. *Cultivating Humanity: A Classical Defense of Reform in Liberal Education*. Cambridge, MA: Harvard University Press.

Osler, Audrey. 2010. 'Citizenship and the Nation-State: Affinity, Identity and Belonging'. In *Globalization, the Nation-State and the Citizen*, edited by Alan Reid, Judith Gill and Alan Sears, 216–222. New York: Routledge.

Osler, Audrey. 2011. 'Education Policy, Social Cohesion and Citizenship'. In *Promoting Social Cohesion: Implications for Policy and Evaluation*, edited by Peter Ratcliffe and Ines Newman, 185–205. Bristol: The Policy Press.

Osler, Audrey. 2016. *Human Rights and Schooling: An Ethical Framework for Teaching for Social Justice, Multicultural Education Series*. New York: Teachers College Press.

Osler, Audrey, and Hugh Starkey. 2005a. *Changing Citizenship: Democracy and Inclusion in Education*. Maidenhead: Open University Press.

Osler, Audrey, and Hugh Starkey. 2005b. 'Study on the Advances in Civic Education in Education Systems: Good Practices in Industrialized Countries'. In *Education for Citizenship and Democracy in a Globalized World: A Comparative Perspective*, edited by Viola Espínola, 19–61. Washington, DC: Integration and Regional Programs Department and Sustainable Development Department.

Osler, Audrey, and Hugh Starkey. 2015. 'Education for Cosmopolitan Citizenship: A Framework for Language Learning'. *Argentinian Journal of Applied Linguistics* 3 (2): 30–39.

Palinscar, AnneMarie, and Ann Brown. 1984. 'Reciprocal Teaching of Comprehension-Fostering and Monitoring Activities'. *Cognition and Instruction* 1: 117–175.

Parekh, Bhikhu. 2000. *The Future of Multi-Ethnic Britain: Report of the Commission on the Future of Multi-Ethnic Britain*. London: Runnymede Trust.

Parker, Walter. 2003. *Teaching Democracy: Unity and Diversity in Public Life*. Edited by James A. Banks, *Multicultural Education Series*. New York: Teachers College Press.

Parker, Walter. 2004. 'Diversity, Globalization, and Democratic Education: Curriculum Possibilities'. In *Diversity and Citizenship Education*, edited by James A. Banks, 433–458. San Fransisco, CA: Jossey-Bass.

Parolin, Gianluca. 2009. *Citizenship in the Arab World: Kin, Religion and Nation-State*. Amsterdam: Amsterdam University Press.

Pettigrew, Thomas F., and Linda R. Tropp. 2011. *When Groups Meet: The Dynamics of Intergroup Contact*. Philadelphia, PA: Psychology Press.

Pocock, John. 1995. 'The Ideal of Citizenship Since Classical Times'. In *Theorizing Citizenship*, edited by Ronald Beiner, 29–52. New York: State University of New York Press.

Pramling, Ingrid. 1990. *Learning to Learn: A Study of Swedish Preschool Children*. New York: Springer-Verlag.

Pratte, Richard. 1988. *The Civic Imperative: Examining the Need for Civic Education*. New York: Teachers College, Columbia University.

Quaynor, Laura. 2012. 'Citizenship Education in Post-Conflict Contexts: A Review of the Literature'. *Education, Citizenship and Social Justice* 7 (1): 33–57. doi: 10.1177/1746197911432593.

Renan, Ernest. 1990. 'What Is a Nation?' In *Nation and Narration*, edited by Homi Bhabha, 8–22. New York: Routledge.

Republic of Lebanon. 1990. Lebanese Constitution as amended in 1990.

Rubin, Beth. 2007. '"There's Still Not Justice": Youth Civic Identity Development Amid Distinct School and Community Contexts'. *Teachers College Record* 109 (2): 449–481.

Ryan, Richard M., and Edward L. Deci. 2000. 'Self-Determination Theory and the Facilitation of Intrinsic Motivation, Social Development, and Well-Being'. *American Psychologist* 55 (1): 68–78. doi: 10.1037/0003-066X.55.1.68.

Sadiki, Larbi. 2004. *The Search for Arab Democracy: Discourses and Counter-Discourses*. London: Hurst & Company.

Said, Edward. 1978. *Orientalism*. Vol. reprinted in 2003. London: Penguin Books.

Salibi, Kamal. 1988. *A House of Many Mansions: The History of Lebanon Reconsidered*. London: I. B. Tauris.

Samaha, Nour. 2006. 'Opposing Youth Movements Take Different Approaches'. *The Daily Star*, 1 December.

Saunders, Harold. 1999. *A Public Peace Process: Sustained Dialogue to Transform Racial and Ethnic Conflicts*. New York: Palgrave.

Sbaiti, Nadya. 2015. '"A Massacre without Precedent": Pedagogical Constituencies and Communities of Knowledge in Mandate Lebanon'. In *The Routledge Handbook of the History of the Middle East Mandates*, edited by Cyrus Schayegh and Andrew Arsan, 321–335. Oxon: Routledge.

Schulz, Wolfram, John Ainley, Tim Friedman, and Petra Lietz. 2011. 'ICCS 2009 Latin American Report: Civic Knowledge and Attitudes among Lower-Secondary Students in Six Latin American Countries'. Amsterdam: IEA. http://pub.iea.nl/fileadmin/user_upload/Publications/Electronic_versions/ICCS_2009_Latin_American_Report.pdf.

Seixas, Peter. 2000. 'Schweigen! die Kinder! or, Does Postmodern History Have a Place in the Schools?' In *Knowing, Teaching, and Learning History: National and International Perspectives*, edited by Peter N. Stearns, Peter C. Seixas and Sam S. Wineburg, 19–37. New York: New York University Press.

Shier, Herry. 2001. 'Pathways to Participation: Openings, Opportunities and Obligations. A New Model for Enhancing Children's Participation in Decision-Making, in Line with Article 13.1 of the UNCRC'. *Children & Society* 15: 107–117. doi: 10.1002/CHI.617.

Shuayb, Maha. 2007. 'Education: A Means for the Cohesion of the Lebanese Confessional Society'. In *Breaking the Cycle: Civil Wars in Lebanon*, edited by Youssef Choueiri, 167–195. London: Stacey International.

Shuayb, Maha. 2015. 'Human Rights and Peace Education in the Lebanese Civics Textbooks'. *Research in Comparative and International Education* 10 (1): 135–150. doi: 10.1177/1745499914567823.

Shuayb, Maha, Bassel Akar, and Nisrine Makkouk. 2011. 'A Whole-School Approach to Active Citizenship and Social Cohesion'. 11th UKFIET International Conference, University of Oxford, Oxford, UK, 14 September.

Siddiqui, Ataullah. 1997. *Christian-Muslim Dialogue in the Twentieth Century*. Hampshire: Macmillan Press Ltd.

Smith, Alan. 2005. 'Education in the Twenty-First Century: Conflict, Reconstruction and Reconciliation'. *Compare: A Journal of Comparative and International Education* 35 (4): 373–391.

Smith, Alan. 2011. 'Education and Peacebuilding: From "Conflict-Analysis" to "Conflict Transformation"'. *FriEnt Essay series* 4: 1–7.

Smith, Alan. 2014. 'Contemporary Challenges for Education in Conflict Affected Countries'. *Journal of International and Comparative Education* 3 (1): 113–125.

Smith, Alan, and Tony Vaux. 2003. *Education, Conflict and International Development*. London: Department for International Development.

Starkey, Hugh. 1992. 'Back to Basic Values: Education for Justice and Peace in the World'. *Journal of Moral Education* 21 (3): 185–192.

Starkey, Hugh. 2012. 'Human Rights, Cosmopolitanism and Utopias: Implications for Citizenship Education'. *Cambridge Journal of Education* 42 (1): 21–35. doi: 10.1080/0305764X.2011.651205.

Starkey, Hugh. 2018. 'Fundamental British Values and Citizenship Education: Tensions Between National and Global Perspectives'. *Geografiska Annaler: Series B, Human Geography* 100 (2): 149–162. doi: 10.1080/04353684.2018.1434420.

Starkey, Hugh, Bassel Akar, Lee Jerome, and Audrey Osler. 2014. 'Power, Pedagogy and Participation: Ethics and Pragmatics in Research with Young People'. *Research in Comparative and International Education* 9 (4): 426–440.

Stenhouse, Lawrence. 1975. *An Introduction to Curriculum Research and Development*. London: Heinemann.

Tabar, Paul. 2009. Immigration and Human Development: Evidence from Lebanon. United Nations Development Program: Human Development Reports.

Tan, Kok-Chor. 2010. 'Nationalism and Cosmopolitanism'. In *The Cosmopolitanism Reader*, edited by Garrett Brown and David Held, 176–190. Cambridge: Polity Press.

Tawil, Sobhi, and Alexandra Harley. 2004. 'Education and Identity-Based Conflict: Assessing Curriculum Policy for Social and Civic Reconstruction'. In *Education, Conflict and Social Cohesion*, edited by Sobhi Tawil and Alexandra Harley, 1–35. Paris: UNESCO, International Bureau of Education.

Ten Dam, Geert, and Monique Volman. 2004. 'Critical Thinking as a Citizenship Competence: Teaching Strategies'. *Learning and Instruction* 14: 359–379.

The Daily Star. 2011. 'Supporters of Hariri, Berri Fight at Beirut University'. *The Daily Star*, 1 November. http://www.dailystar.com.lb/News/Politics/2011/Nov-01/152795-student-supporters-of-hariri-berri-fight-at-beirut-university.ashx#axzz1nDPB1sCz.

Thomas, Kenneth W., and Betty A. Velthouse. 1990. 'Cognitive Elements of Empowerment: An "Interpretive" Model of Intrinsic Task Motivation'. *The Academy of Management Review* 15 (4): 666–681. doi: 10.2307/258687.

Tibi, Bassam. 1997. *Arab Nationalism: Between Islam and the Nation-State.* Third ed. London: Macmillan Press.

Tibi, Bassam. 2004. 'Education and Democratization in an Age of Islamism'. In *Educating for Democracy: Paideia in an Age of Uncertainty*, edited by Alan M. Olson, David M. Steiner and Irina S. Tuuli, 203–220. Lanham, MD: Rowman Littlefield Publishers.

Tolmie, Andrew Kenneth, Keith J. Topping, Donald Christie, Caroline Donaldson, Christine Howe, Emma Jessiman, Kay Livingston, and Allen Thurston. 2010. 'Social Effects of Collaborative Learning in Primary Schools'. *Learning and Instruction* 20 (3): 177–191. doi: https://doi.org/10.1016/j.learninstruc.2009.01.005.

Tomaševski, Katarina. 2001. 'Human Rights Obligations: Making Education Available, Accessible, Acceptable, and Adaptable'. *Right to Education Primers* 3. http://www.right-to-education.org/sites/right-to-education.org/files/resource-attachments/Tomasevski_Primer%203.pdf.

Transparency International. 2015. *Corruption Perceptions Index 2015.* http://www.transparency.org/cpi2015.

Transparency International. 2018. *Corruption Perceptions Index 2017.* https://www.transparency.org/news/feature/corruption_perceptions_index_2017.

Treseder, Phil. 1997. *Empowering Children and Young People: Training Manual.* London: Save the Children and Children's Rights Office.

Turner, Bryan. 1990. 'Outline of a Theory of Citizenship'. *Sociology of Health and Illness* 24 (2): 189–218.

Turner, Bryan. 1997. 'Citizenship Studies: A General Theory'. *Citizenship Studies* 1 (1): 5–18. doi: 10.1080/13621029708420644.

UNCT. 2009. United Nations Development Assistance Framework Lebanon (2010–2014). Beirut: United Nations. Retrieved 1 November 2010. http://planipolis.iiep.unesco.org/en/2009/united-nations-development-assistance-framework-undaf-lebanon-2010-2014-4829.

UNDP, MEHE, and CDR. 2008. Education and Citizenship: Concepts, Attitudes, Skills and Actions: Analysis of Survey Results of 9th Grade Students in Lebanon. Beirut: UNDP.

UNESCO. 2011. *Education for All Global Monitoring Report: The Hidden Crisis: Armed Conflict and Education.* Paris: UNESCO.

UNESCO. 2015. 'Education for All 2000–2015: Achievements and Challenges'. Paris: UNESCO. http://unesdoc.unesco.org/images/0023/002322/232205e.pdf.

UNESCO IBE. 2011. Conflict and Education: A List of Resources, No. 2 (revised 2012). UNESCO and the International Bureau of Education. http://www.ibe.unesco.org/fileadmin/user_upload/Documentation/Special-Search/2012Conflictdoc.pdf.

UNHCR. 2016. 'Global Trends: Forced Displacement in 2015'. Geneva: UNHCR. http://www.unhcr.org/576408cd7.

UNICEF. 2011. *The Role of Education in Peacebuilding: A Literature Review*. New York: United Nations Children's Fund.

United Nations. 1989. *Convention on the Rights of the Child*. Geneva: United Nations.

UNRWA. 2017. 'Where We Work: Lebanon'. http://www.unrwa.org/where-we-work/lebanon.

Ury, William. 2000. *The Third Side: Why We Fight and How We Can Stop*. Revised ed. New York: Penguin.

Van der Ploeg, Piet, and Laurence Guérin. 2016. 'Questioning Participation and Solidarity as Goals of Citizenship Education'. *Critical Review* 28 (2): 248–264. doi: 10.1080/08913811.2016.1191191.

Vansteenkiste, Maarten, Willy Lens, and Edward L. Deci. 2006. 'Intrinsic versus Extrinsic Goal Contents in Self-Determination Theory: Another Look at the Quality of Academic Motivation'. *Educational Psychologist* 41 (1): 19–31. doi: 10.1207/s15326985ep4101_4.

Vavrus, Michael. 2012. 'Diversity: A Contested Concept (Perspectives in Education)'. In *Encyclopedia of Diversity in Education*, edited by James Banks. Thousand Oaks, CA: Sage.

Verhellen, Eugeen. 2000. 'Children's Rights and Education'. In *Citizenship and Democracy in Schools: Diversity, Identity, Equality*, edited by Audrey Osler, 33–43. Stoke on Trent: Trentham.

Vongalis-Macrow, Athena. 2006. 'Rebuilding Regimes or Rebuilding Community? Teachers' Agency for Social Reconstruction in Iraq'. *Journal of Peace Education* 3 (1): 99–113.

Walter, James, and Margaret MacLeod. 2002. *The Citizens' Bargain: A Documentary History of Australian Views since 1890*. Sydney: UNSW Press.

Walzer, Michael. 1989. 'Citizenship'. In *Political Innovation and Conceptual Change*, edited by Terence Ball, James Farr and Russell L. Hanson, 211–219. Cambridge: Cambridge University Press.

Watkins, Chris. 2005. *Classrooms as Learning Communities: What's in It for Schools?, What's in It for Schools?* London: Routledge.

Watkins, Chris. 2015. 'Meta-Learning in Classrooms'. In *The SAGE Handbook of Learning*, edited by David Scott and Eleanore Hargreaves, 321–330. London: Sage.

Watkins, Chris, Eileen Carnell, and Caroline Lodge. 2007. *Effective Learning in Classrooms*. London: Paul Chapman.

Watkins, Chris, Eileen Carnell, Caroline Lodge, Patsy Wagner, and Caroline Whalley. 2001. 'Learning about Learning Enhances Performance'. *NSIN Research Matters* (13): 1–8.

Watt, William Montgomery. 1979. *What Is Islam?* Second ed. London: Longman.

Wegerif, Rupert. 2008. 'Dialogic or Dialectic? The Significance of Ontological Assumptions in Research on Educational Dialogue'. *British Educational Research Journal* 34 (3): 347–361.

Wegerif, Rupert, Neil Mercer, and Lyn Dawes. 1999. 'From Social Interaction to Individual Reasoning: An Empirical Investigation of a Possible Socio-Cultural Model of Cognitive Development'. *Learning and Instruction* 9 (6): 493–516. doi: https://doi.org/10.1016/S0959-4752(99)00013-4.

Weinstein, Harvey M., Sarah W. Freedman, and Holly Hughson. 2007. 'School Voices: Challenges Facing Education Systems after Identity-Based Conflicts'. *Education, Citizenship and Social Justice* 2 (1): 41–71.

Weller, Susie. 2007. *Teenagers' Citizenship*. Oxon: Routledge.

Wingo, Ajume. 2006. 'Joy in Living Together: Toward a Civic Appreciation of Laughter'. *The Journal of Political Philosophy* 14 (2): 186–202.

Zakharia, Zeena. 2011. The Role of Education in Peacebuilding: Case Study – Lebanon. New York: UNICEF.

Zembylas, Michalinos, Constadina Charalambous, Panayiota Charalambous, and Panayiota Kendeou. 2011. 'Promoting Peaceful Coexistence in Conflict-Ridden Cyprus: Teachers' Difficulties and Emotions towards a New Policy Initiative'. *Teaching and Teacher Education* 27 (2): 332–341. doi: https://doi.org/10.1016/j.tate.2010.08.015.

Zembylas, Michalinos, and Froso Kambani. 2012. 'The Teaching of Controversial Issues during Elementary-Level History Instruction: Greek-Cypriot Teachers' Perceptions and Emotions'. *Theory & Research in Social Education* 40 (2): 107–133. doi: 10.1080/00933104.2012.670591.

Zoreik, Aisha. 2000. *Civics Education: How Do We Deal with It*. Beirut: Arab Scientific Publishers.

Zubaida, Sami. 2002. 'Middle Eastern Experiences of Cosmopolitanism'. In *Conceiving Cosmopolitanism: Theory, Context, and Practice*, edited by Steven Vertovec and Robin Cohen, 32–41. Oxford: Oxford University Press.

Index

active citizenship 29–32, 44–5
assessment 16, 59, 111–13
    effect on learning 17, 58, 81, 98–9, 108, 113, 117, 122–3
    low-stakes status 111–12, 128
    official exams 64–5, 77, 112, 115

citizenship
    Arab and Islamic 36–8
    elements of 27–9
    principles 32–3
    relationship with communities 26–7
    symbols 104
citizenship education 22
    curricula in Lebanon 77–9, 80–1
    informal through civil society 85, 94
    informal through home 116–17
    young people's model of 94–6
citizenship education reform
    high-impact teachers 143–7
    top-down failures 140–3
civic education
    catch-22 135–7
    in relation to citizenship education 133–5
classrooms. See learning
communitarianism 92–3
community service 56, 96, 101, 131–2, 134, 142–3
conflict
    conflict-affected 10–13
    constructive and destructive expressions 11, 13, 22–3, 57
    in Lebanon 2, 70–5
    themes in citizenship education curriculum 96–7
cosmopolitanism 34, 42, 43, 130–1
    Arab discourse 39–41
    and nationalism. See nationalism
curriculum
    essentialism 48, 58
    extra-curricular 56, 93
    horizontal 109

prescriptive 123, 135
process 16, 48, 78, 142
reform by governments 20, 77–8, 129–30, 140–1
review of Lebanese civics curriculum 78–81
teachers as curriculum makers 54, 144–7

Dewey, John 15, 48, 49, 54–5, 133
dialogue
    classroom learning 97, 100, 110, 107, 118–20
    in the classroom on politics 115–16
    dialogic pedagogy 58–9, 108, 132–3
    procedures for debates 119–20
    rhetorical dialogues 58, 114
diamond ranking 83, 84
diversity 1–2, 13–14, 21, 23, 71, 103, 116

education
    aims for development 3, 14, 15, 21–2, 76
    children's rights 14, 17
    do no harm 19
    as harm 15–17, 18, 19
    emotionality 59–60, 89–90, 98, 113, 118–19, 128–9
    essentialism 55

Freire, Paulo 44, 57–8, 133

gender equality 87, 90

Hart's ladder 56, 143
history education 20, 100, 143
human rights
    Arab discourse 41–2
    Lebanon 76

language 16, 20, 33, 38, 43, 50, 52, 56, 64–5, 77, 79–80, 99–100, 111, 115, 127, 130–1

learning
　　active learning 49
　　Arab and Islamic traditions of 61–3
　　banking as knowledge transference
　　　　107, 110, 123, 131–2
　　collaborative learning 50–1
　　learner-driven learning 53–4
　　meta-learning 51–3
　　participation 54–6
　　politics of 64–5
　　rote (*see* memorization)
　　safe classroom environment 19, 22–3, 47
learning to live together 17, 48

memorization 16, 20, 81, 134, 135, 139
　　Arab and Islamic traditions of 62–5
　　barrier to learner responsibility
　　　　112–13, 122, 131
　　students' experiences 96, 98–100
　　teachers' approaches 107–8, 110,
　　　　112–13, 115, 122–3
　　undermining active citizenship 99, 122–3

nationalism 12, 21, 78, 104
　　Arab nationalism 38

　　in citizenship education 60, 105,
　　　　129–130, 133–4
　　and cosmopolitanism 34, 40, 42–3,
　　　　105
　　dangers of 33, 35, 111
　　education reform 64, 77–8
　　in history education 16
　　and post-colonialism 38–9
　　in teachers' constructs of citizenship
　　　　104–6

post-conflict. *See* conflict-affected
pragmatism 48, 55–6

refugees 1, 14, 16, 18, 28, 31, 32, 35, 72–3,
　　85, 103

textbook
　　as government text 77, 78, 80–1
　　when learning and teaching 99–100,
　　　　109–11, 114–17, 121, 123, 127–8,
　　　　136
theory of change. *See* citizenship
　　education reform